Six Con...

Over Five Decades

An Intrepid Woman's Memoir

Karen Christie

Dear Colin,

Enjoy the journey!

xoxo

Karen Christie

Reciprocity Publishing
Victoria BC, Canada

Six Continents Over Five Decades:
An Intrepid Woman's Memoir

Citation: Christie, Karen. *Six continents over five decades: An intrepid woman's memoir.* Victoria, BC: Reciprocity Publishing, 2022.

Cover photo by fellow cyclist Pauline, Bali, 1979
Author photo by Elizabeth M. Campa, Haiti, 2015
World map: Miller projection map from Wikimedia.org, CC
Cover and Book Design: Daniel Doherty, Reciprocity Publishing

Published in Canada by Reciprocity Publishing
www.reciprocitypublishing.com

ISBN: 978-1-928114-46-8 (paperback)
978-1-928114-47-5 (electronic book)

1st Edition: December 2022

Printed in Canada 10 9 8 7 6 5 4 3 2

To my mother
Barbara Christie
1927 - 2020

Contents

Photographs   vi
World Map   viii
Acknowledgements   xi

EPISODE I My First Two Decades in North America   1
1. Family   1

EPISODE II My 20s in Europe, North America, Australia and Asia   9
2. Heading Overseas to Norway   11
3. Yukon to Australia   19
4. En Route Down Under   29
5. An Asian Cycling Lesson   35
6. More Cycling in Asia   39

EPISODE III My 30s in North America and Africa   47
7. Teaching in Calgary   49
8. Teaching in Ethiopia   53
9. Changing Careers   71

EPISODE IV My 40s in North & South America and Europe   77
10. Working with NGOs in Ottawa   79
11. Shifting Gears to a Multilateral Organization   87
12. Assignment #2 in Bosnia   95
13. Assignments in the Serbian Republic   101
14. The Federation of Bosnia and Hercegovina   105

EPISODE V My 50s in Europe and Asia   121
15. More in the Former Yugoslavia   123
16. Expertise in Election Administration   135
17. Re-inventing Myself, Again!   141
18. Being a Federal Public Servant in Ottawa   145
19. First Posting with the Government of Canada   155
20. Kandahar, Afghanistan   163

EPISODE VI My 60s in Asia and Haiti   177
21. Three More Years on the Afghanistan Program   179
22. The Sunny Caribbean   195
Epilogue   217
About the Author   219

Photographs

EPISODE I: My 1st 20 years
Dedication
  Mum and me, 1953
  Mum at Barbara Christie Needle Arts in Calgary
Chapter 1
  Mum, Dad and me en route from Toronto to Calgary, April 1950
  Dad and me, 1953
  High school graduation, 1967

EPISODE II: My 20s
Chapter 2
  Strawberry picking, Norway
  With the Haug family on the school boat
  Cycling in Norway, 1981
Chapter 3
  With my students in Dawson City, mid 1970s
  Yukon River canoe trip, 1976
Chapter 4
  Summiting Ayers Rock, Australia, 1979
  On the Heaphy Track, NZ
Chapter 6
  Cycling in Korea, 1979
  Cycling in Bali, 1979

EPISODE III: My 30s
Chapter 7
  With my ESL class at Queen Elizabeth Jr/Sr High School, Calgary
  Hiking with ESL students on Tunnel Mountain, Banff, Alberta
  Field trip to Expo 86, Vancouver, Canada
Chapter 8
  Arba Minch Water Technology Institute (AWTI), 1987-88
  AWTI colleagues, Ethiopia
  In the AWTI classroom
  Promoting women in Ethiopia
Chapter 9
  Ready to drive from Calgary to Ottawa, 1989

EPISODE IV: My 40s
   Chapter 10
      WUSC office in Ottawa, mid 1990s
   Chapter 12
      With colleagues and host family, Maglaj, Bosnia 1997
      Voter registration in Maglaj
      Destroyed building, Maglaj
   Chapter 14
      Neretva River, Mostar, Bosnia and Herzegovina
      With Sadeta and Zoran overlooking Mostar
      'Benetton babe' with friend Rob
      Reunited with Martino – from Ethiopia to Bosnia Hercegovina

EPISODE V: My 50s
   Chapter 15
      Field trip with OSCE vehicle, Kosovo
      Receiving UN Peacekeeping Medal from MP Mauril Belanger, 2005
      Forest fire, on vacation in Montenegro
   Chapter 20
      Kandahar Provincial Reconstruction Team (KPRT), Afghanistan
      Adrenalin junkie in a Cougar helicopter
      With Canadian Forces colleague, my KPRT office
      Women's *shura* at KPRT
      KPRT 'reservoir' at January 1st fundraiser

EPISODE VI: My 60s
   Chapter 21
      My 'blast-pod' in Kabul, Afghanistan, at the door...inside
      Socializing on blast-pod deck
      With Afghan Minister of Education, 2011
      With RCMP on Remembrance Day, 2011
      Colleagues and Gov. General David Johnston, Christmas Eve, 2011
      Our education team visit to Herat, Afghanistan, 2012
      School girls in Herat
   Chapter 22
      Snacks on spa day at my residence in Port-au-Prince, Haiti
      Receiving my 3rd medal at the Canadian Embassy in Haiti
      With Dad, showing off our 5 medals
      Enjoying Cote des Arcadins, north of Port-au-Prince
      Club Indigo, Cote des Arcadins
      Pam and me at Cyvadier Plage near Jacmel, Haiti
      Spa day at my residence in Port-au-Prince
      The stairs where I broke my arm, Port-au-Prince
      Haitian police plaque from, my Embassy office
      Happy camper portrait after almost 3 years in Haiti, 2015
   Epilogue
      'Refirement', where the livin' is easy! Cowichan River, Canada

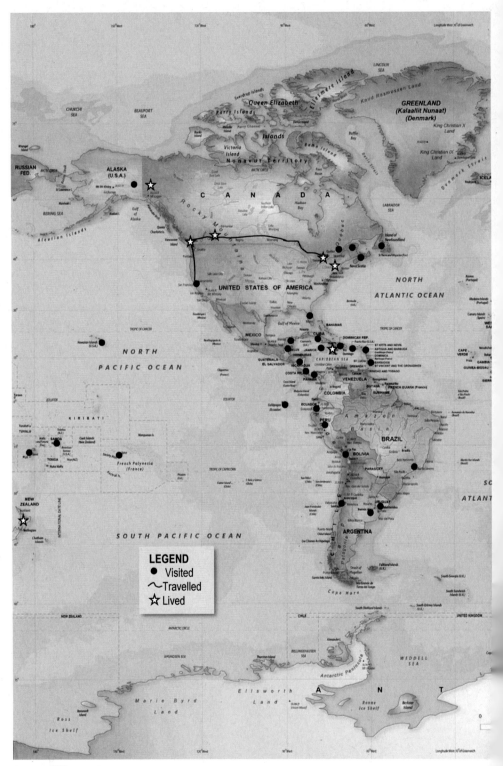

LEGEND
● Visited
〜 Travelled
☆ Lived

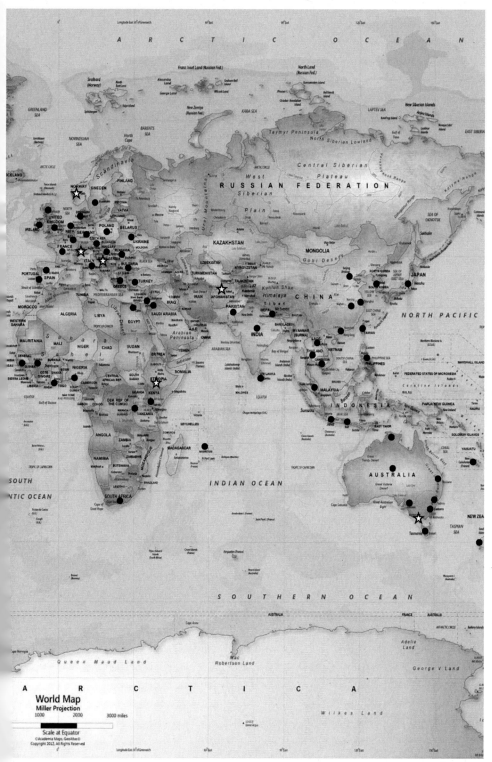

Acknowledgements

It is with love and great affection that I express my heartfelt gratitude to my dear mother for asking me to write my life story. I read her some chapters of the book as I was writing them. She often told me she couldn't work out where I came from, because I became such a wanderer. But she too had a spirit of adventure as you will read in the first chapter.

I would also like to thank Faye Ferguson who helped me get this writing project started through her course entitled, Chronicling your Life Story, offered by the University of Victoria's Extension Program. There I met others with the same objective, to tell their life story. After the course ended, some of us continued to get together on a monthly basis to read our latest efforts to each other for support, encouragement and motivation.

One of our fellow writers was Merry Connor who hosted us each month in 2018-19. Sadly, we lost Merry to an extremely aggressive brain tumour in June 2019. Merry's work was exquisitely done and so we chose to call ourselves the Merry Connor Writers' Group. We fondly remember her and her stories.

I would like to acknowledge I have been inspired by others who have managed to publish their stories. Three people come to mind – two from my professional life, and one from my teenage years. I am pretty good at staying connected with the many people who have crossed my path through the years. One in particular resurfaced in November 2019 and told me about the memoir of my high school buddy, Eve Crawford. On the one hand I was delighted to hear this news, but I will confess to being slightly chagrined that Eve had pulled it together and got her story out there before I did!

Then of course I acknowledge the wonderful friends who have supported me. Janice Logan, a friend who is a professional editor, was the first to read my entire manuscript in order to provide me with a comprehensive structural review. I am exceedingly grateful to her for this generous gift. Other friends listened as I whined about the struggle to fine tune my work and actually get it between these covers. Sincere thanks to all of you for caring, and for waiting patiently for your turn to read the result!

This chronicle of my life is about both people and place, and the rich experiences they provided me around the world. Every decade starting with my twenties featured huge life opportunities which I embraced with enthusiasm.

Adventure lies ahead. As one of Canada's former prime ministers, Jean Chrétien, once said, "Fasten your seatbelts; it's going to be one hell of a ride!" I trust that I will rise to the occasion and meet your expectations.

Without further ado, here it is, also in part thanks to Covid-19 which gave me the gift of time at home so I could finish this!

EPISODE I

My First Two Decades in North America

1. Family

In the first 66 years of my life, I lived and worked on six continents, moving at least 32 times. Finally, in October 2016 I made what I hope will be my last move, from Canada's capital city, Ottawa, to Victoria, a provincial capital city on the west coast of British Columbia (BC). Here in the beautiful region of Cascadia, as it is also known, I am learning some of the ways of the Indigenous peoples. This tendency has been a feature of my wandering life, becoming familiar with the culture in which I find myself. It is the custom of the Indigenous peoples, when introducing themselves, to provide their ancestral history so I have chosen to open my story in that way.

On both sides of my family, I am descended from Scots who came to Canada in the 1800s, making me a sixth generation Canadian on my mother's side, and fifth generation on my father's. The earlier arrival on these shores was a military officer, and the latter was a baker. In tracing these origins, I could not help but notice the lineage comes primarily from the male family members but of course men do not change their surnames when they marry, making it easier to trace them.

To this day, I have an old sea chest my maternal great, great, great grandfather brought to the New World. Alexander Browne Baxter was born in Edinburgh, Scotland in 1790. Fortunately, I have a nine-page record written by him in 1859. It describes his arrival, via New York City, in the Township of Moore in Upper Canada in 1835. He was a military man, both tactical and later as an adjutant, he became paymaster of the Corps.

On my father's side, I can trace my roots to my great, great grandfather, William Mellis Christie, who came to Toronto in 1848 at the age of 19 from Huntley, Scotland. He had already completed his apprenticeship as a baker, and so began Christie's Biscuits. Mr. Christie would roll a trolley of baked goods either along Yonge or Bloor Streets (I have read both!) to get the business going. My father was scarcely a year old when Christie's Biscuits was sold to Nabisco in 1928.

My paternal grandmother, Katherine Burruss, married into the Christie family in the early 1920s. She would react to the jingle that came out in the 1980s, "Mr. Christie, you make good cookies," saying that my great, great grandfather would have been so proud to have heard that popular line about him and his company.

I was a teacher in the early years of my career and when I introduced myself to the students as Miss Christie, I was always asked, "Do you make good cookies?" I found telling them the family story was a great icebreaker.

My father, Robert (Bob) Burruss Christie, and mother, Barbara (Barbie) Brooke Baxter, married in 1949, the same year I was born. I was just four months old in the spring of 1950 when my parents, Dad at age 25 and Mum just 23, drove from Toronto, where all three of us were born, across Canada to Calgary. I have a photo of their grey Chevy, and the caravan trailer they towed for bedding down at night. And I wonder where I might have got my wandering spirit? Ask no further! I spent my first night in Calgary in a drawer at a downtown hotel. The seeds of my innate wanderlust had been sown, unbeknownst to me. Although my father had the pioneer spirit to take on this challenge of moving his young family out west in the early 1950s, he then remained in Calgary for the rest of his life, which ended in October 2015, three weeks short of his 90th birthday.

I grew up in the 1950s and 1960s in a relatively conservative Calgary family but I became a bit of a flower child in my late teenage years and went through an anti-establishment phase. By the time I was in my early twenties, my father was affectionately calling me a *pinko*, given that I leaned to the left, in contrast to him. He would become a card-carrying member of the Alberta Reform Party during its time. Fortunately, I was not offended by the label Dad had given me, perhaps even taking it as a compliment!

I was close to my father in some ways but less so in others, and occasionally more than others. It is often that way, I think. He bonded with his children on the ski hill. My earliest memories are when I was six and my only brother at that time, Liam, was three. My dad would take us to the hill on the first hole of the Calgary Golf and Country Club to teach us to ski. We had what were called *bear trap bindings* and plain old over-boots that fitted over our shoes. These outings were relatively frequent, despite the temper tantrums my brother threw. Liam is now a level 4 (out of 5) ski instructor, which means he is qualified to train ski instructors. I never entered that realm of expertise but I did enjoy skiing in our almost-backyard, the Canadian Rocky Mountains near Banff and Lake Louise.

I abandoned my skis in my mid-fifties due to joint issues, but those years of skiing were strong bonding times with my father. My mother missed out as she was not at all athletic. My one memory of her on the ski hill was when she rode piggyback as my dad was skiing down the Bow Glacier. As the story goes, my mother was laughing so hard she wet her pants! Skiing was an activity that brought some of the family together but in the process, it isolated my mother. My dad skied consecutively for some 78 winters, from age six in the Laurentians near Montreal to age 82 in the Rockies. He always used to say, "Skiing is not a sport; it is a way of life."

As is often the case, my parents were very different people. I have strong memories of being my mother's little helper. I was the only girl and I was the oldest. I had three younger brothers whom I adored. The youngest, Tom, was born when I was 11 and a half, and as I never had children of my own, which of course I didn't know then, he was to some extent like my child. At any rate, I was quite a mature and responsible 12-year-old. I was also tall for my age (Dad was six foot two), and so I was often mistaken in my teen years as being older.

My mother showered us all with love and often praised me. I recognize that as an adult, I have always had a positive response to praise. Who doesn't, I suppose? I can definitely say that I feel blessed by my family of origin and the wonderful country where I was born. My parents provided for me very well and for that I am most grateful. I am aware this makes me a person of privilege. I know my father worked hard for what we had and so did my grandparents on both sides. My mother told me her father, Thomas Alexander Baxter, had sold pots and pans door to door during the Great Depression. That grandfather set up a fund for me as a child for my post-secondary education. Thanks to that generous gift, I began my working life without debt and hence could pursue my young dreams.

But back to Mum who was quite a joyful, energetic person in her own way. She loved to sing and had a lovely voice she would use with enthusiasm. I will always remember the first time as an adult I heard the classic version of *Wunderbar*. It was almost unrecognizable as my mother used to belt it out with gusto as she lovingly prepared our family meals. But I later learned it was really more of a lilting love song, meant to be sung gently and softly! I never would have guessed.

I am aware that although my family had a strong influence on my life, I am affected by place as well. Skiing with my father and brothers gave me a love of the outdoors. My father also provided another venue where we had quality time – at the family cottage in Georgian Bay where he had spent time as a teenager. I spent summers there from a very early age, four or five, I think. It meant trips across Canada to get there by car, train or plane, and all the memories associated with those journeys – such as losing my wallet on the train when my brother Liam and I traveled across the country alone when I was a teenager!

My maternal grandmother also had a cottage on Georgian Bay although I think it was only until my early teens. It was on the mainland at a place called Cedar Point which looked out over white sandy beaches and clear blue waters to Christian Island. I learned to play canasta there and although it is a game of the past, I still enjoy board games. There is a chance it might have something to do with my competitive spirit which is alive and well to this day.

I cherished my time at the Georgian Bay and I always will. Sadly, my father's cottage is no longer in the family but in the hands of my Toronto cousins with whom we spent the summers. For many of my adult years, I lived in Ottawa and so was able to drive over to the Bay, as we called it, in just a few hours. This further solidified my relationship with my father in the 1990s and until he stopped going there in the mid to late 2000s.

I married young, at the age of 22 in 1972, and divorced quite soon thereafter, at 24. It was my choice although I disliked breaking my marriage vows. I

5

almost married a second time, some 23 years later but, fortunately, I paid attention to my cold feet and ended the engagement in time.

I come from a family of frequent divorces, going back to both my maternal and paternal grandparents. It might be fair to say that the odds were stacked against me in that regard. Nevertheless, I have always been someone who considers the glass half-full so I have usually made the best of any situation.

For example, I had four sets of grandparents, which meant many more gifts at Christmas and birthdays. I had just turned 21 when I found out my parents were separating. It was not a surprise. It was obvious my parents were not made for each other so it was probably best they moved on with their lives as separate entities. My father remarried within six months and was still married to my stepmother when he died some 44 years later. My mother was a different story, although happily she did eventually end up with a lovely man. Sadly, though, he was 22 years her senior and he has been gone now for over 20 years.

There were both positive and negative aspects of our broken family. I spent over four decades of my adult life dividing my family time between my mother and father – at Christmas and during summer holidays. On the brighter side, I learned in my early twenties that if you discovered you didn't want to have children with the person you married, perhaps it was not a good idea to remain married to that person. I knew all too well it was not wise to bring children into a dysfunctional marriage. That being said, my memory is that I grew up in a loving home.

There were many benefits, from my perspective, to no longer being married at the age of 24. I had just completed an additional year at university to get my teacher's certificate and, being single, I felt the world was my oyster. At that age, I had already traveled to

Europe, where I stayed for 16 months, working in Norway and Switzerland on a farm and in a hotel respectively. Subsequently, I worked in the US for a year. At that point I already considered myself a veteran traveler so I wondered where else I wanted to explore. Look out, world, here I come!

EPISODE II

My 20s in Europe, North America, Australia and Asia

2. Heading Overseas to Norway

People with inquiring minds occasionally ask me how I ended up working internationally. I reply it was likely destiny and it's not easy to define.

I mentioned it was my parents' pioneering spirit that infected me with wanderlust. So be it. In my eyes it is a tale to be told – from sleeping as an infant in a drawer in a downtown Calgary hotel to representing Canada at our embassy in Haiti at the end of my career, 62 years later.

I have also mentioned the importance of place, which is what the 37 years of my working life entail. Each of these places has created who I am today.

My first overseas experience was on a farm in Norway at the age of 20. I had graduated with a Bachelor of Arts from the University of Alberta in Edmonton in 1970 when the adventures began. Family and friends teased me that I had earned a BA, majoring in French with an Italian minor, to go and pitch BS in Norway the first summer after graduation. Au contraire, in fact, as I was lucky enough to land at a fruit farm where I picked strawberries for days on end, enjoying the fresh succulent berries whenever I wished. Later it would be pears and I dreamt about the bulbous golden globes filling my hands as I picked them and gently laid them in baskets.

But I would like to backtrack slightly in order to tell you about the journey to Norway. This opportunity arose long before the internet. The student information office on campus must have been where I found a brochure about working in Norway. That last year at university, I had studied Norwegian. Why, you might ask. Truth be told, it was because the older sister of a

11

good friend in Calgary had married a tall, handsome Norwegian man and that was reason enough!

That first trans-Atlantic trip was long and continued all the way to Oslo. From there I took a train, boats and buses to reach Sognefjord, the longest fjord in the country. En route, stopping overnight in the town of Voss, my first words to the train conductor were not in the language I had studied, but in my own tongue as I was so tired, "Do you speak English?" I needed help finding a place to rest my weary head that evening. He kindly directed me to an appropriate shelter.

At the end of this mini-marathon, which is what it felt like, I was met by the farmer, 48-year-old Anders Haug, who rowed me across the fjord to the farm at Fimreite as there were no roads on the south side of the fjord. His family was anxiously awaiting my arrival: his wife Ester, their seven children ranging in age from 20 to 11, and his mother who was 76. I later learned this older woman could still row across the fjord, which amazed me because being only 20 myself, she looked ancient!

Fortunately, I bonded quickly with the family, who welcomed me warmly despite some trepidation on their part, I later learned, that I would be suitable. The biggest initial challenge and quite a surprise was that the children wanted to practice the English they had learned in school. I, however, was determined to use my newly acquired Norwegian. Eventually, I prevailed but with numerous bouts of laughter over the mistakes I made. One that stays with me still, some 50 years later, is when I asked, "Kan du kvelpe meg?" I was trying to ask for help but apparently, I had used the wrong verb which referred to the physical act of a female dog giving birth!

The other intriguing thing at the time was to discover I had learned *Bokmål*, which is formal

Norwegian and what the children would have learned at school. In this rural part of the country closer to its west coast, the common tongue was *Nynorsk* (New Norwegian). It made the parents smile as they heard their children speaking to me in their formal language. Although it was summer when I was there and school was out, I learned the children went to school on a school boat.

Another vivid memory from my stay of two and a half months was the unusual form of play. It was tickling! The boys would go so far as to tickle their mother, who was 52, on the kitchen floor! If my brothers had done this to my mother, there would have been hell to pay. I was not spared the experience either; I can remember thinking I would die of laughter! Those were good times for sure and really carefree.

It is worth noting there was no indoor plumbing. Rather, we used an outhouse and for toilet paper there was only newspaper. I will say no more about that except to add that we had a bath only once a week. Buckets of water were heated and poured into a bathtub which needed plumbing fixtures and running water, things we took for granted in Canada in 1970.

On the weekends, we hiked up the big hill behind the farm to explore the vast green pastures where livestock grazed. I remember the Haug children scrambled up there with the agility of goats whereas I was hard pressed to catch my breath to keep up to them. In my teens in the 1960s, physical fitness was not as important as it is now. My face was red from the exertion, but it was worth the effort for the glorious views of the majestic fjord to the east and west, and the rich landscapes sloping down to it.

Another form of entertainment was jumping into the fjord on a hot summer's day. That was more my speed, as I have always thought of myself as being part

13

fish. My moon sign is in the water sign of Pisces, and my sun in Capricorn, an earth sign. I must say the fjord was very cold, but it brought back memories of being in the refreshing waters of the Georgian Bay in my childhood. What a great, yet simple way to enjoy ourselves, in the beautiful country surrounding us.

Another aspect of Norwegian rural culture was the food. On the farm we ate small crepes, as we in Canada would eat bread, about three times a day. We put butter and sugar or jam on them and rolled them up. They were delicious. This was not the case for the hard brown goat cheese, *geitost*, for which I never developed a liking. The meal I really did not like was cubes of bacon in a thick white sauce over boiled potatoes. The main meal was served at midday to sustain the farmer, Anders, and his children who served as his crew doing hard physical labour. Ester too worked exceedingly hard inside the house for the most part, ensuring we all had sufficient fuel to get the work done. Of course, many other household chores had to be done and her daughters provided valuable support. It was certainly a team effort.

Alcohol was not part of everyday life on the farm although it was available in the form of a very strong local brew, something like aquavit. I have never been a big drinker and alcohol affects me quite quickly. I did have an adventure on the farm, though. After about five or six weeks of picking strawberries, I was invited to travel with Anders in a small, motorized boat up the fjord to deliver the harvest. I have always loved being on the water and this was no exception. On arriving at our destination, I was offered some local alcohol, which I accepted. Oh my, was it strong, especially after not having drunk any alcohol for all that time and on a relatively empty stomach. I suffered no harm, but I do remember having a very light head.

My first summer adventure with the Haug family ended with the visit of two girlfriends from the University of Alberta. They had started their European travel experience and stopped in at the farm to help for a few days. Then I left with them and we hitchhiked to Munich for October Fest. There I met an American family who took a liking to me and asked me to look after their children while they went on a three-week trip back to the States. I enjoyed the opportunity to spend more time in that part of Germany. My European experience was gradually expanding in an unexpected way and I was learning to go with the flow. My desire to learn by doing was fueled by the adventure as it evolved.

After Bavaria, I continued my travels on my own and in Switzerland, met Bill, the American man with whom I later lived in Boston, eventually married in Calgary, and subsequently divorced. We lived and worked in Grindelwald in the shadow of the great Eiger Mountain for about four months during the winter of 1970 and 1971. I was what I called in those days a 'char' – cleaning rooms, sinks, showers and toilets in a small hotel while Bill had similar jobs at the nearby youth hostel.

We eventually broke loose, with our hard-earned francs in our pockets, to hitchhike and camp around Europe. This wandering culminated in a visit to the Haug farm for a month the following summer, 1971. At that time, I promised the kids of the Norwegian family I would return to visit them in ten years. We all found that to be hilariously funny, thinking about how old we would all be by then (just 31 in my case!)

I am happy to report that I did return in 1981 as promised, but solo and on a bicycle, which led to quite an interesting journey. By that time, I had traveled widely in Asia, also on a bicycle, and so had been exposed to many other cultures. With that newly acquired basis of comparison, I found the Norwegians rather closed and cold, quite the opposite of what I had experienced on the family farm. I am convinced climate plays a role in the character of people in a nation. It has been my experience that people in warmer countries tend to be more open and friendly, whereas those from colder climes can be the opposite.

To confound this reality further in Norway in 1981 was the fact I was clearly a stranger and yet this outsider spoke some version of the local language, which added another layer of confusion. Nevertheless, I managed to arrive at the farm without too much difficulty – with one exception. The roads in Norway feature long tunnels and I was not prepared for this. I did not have bike lights since I had not planned to cycle after dark. I waited at the entrance to a tunnel (of a kilometre or more) for a car to drive through so I could follow the lights and not get hit by other cars. Clearly, I survived.

For a few years after my adventures with the Haugs, I sent Christmas cards to try to keep my Norwegian alive as no tall handsome Norwegian had stepped forward to marry me! I have stayed in touch with the oldest daughter, Magni, who married an Englishman. They lived in England for a few years but have now retired and moved back to the family farm in Norway.

The youngest child, Ase, found me through social media in the summer of 2011. Two of her sons had been awarded a hockey scholarship to Canada and she was hoping we might meet. Sadly, it was not to be as I was posted to our embassy in Kabul, Afghanistan and so was not able to welcome her to my country as her family had done for me some forty years earlier.

My Norwegian connections continued throughout my life. In particular, when I was teaching in rural Ethiopia, I met a Norwegian family working in a mission hospital, one of the best in the country. I will always remember greeting Norwegian visitors of theirs in their own language. They were especially confused to meet a non-Norwegian who spoke their language in Ethiopia! This is a great example of why I wanted to study languages – to open up my world. I had a good start on making that a reality. Knowing other languages enriches the experience of new places.

3. Yukon to Australia

Languages were not my sole passion. I have mentioned I was a skier, thanks to my father's devotion to the sport or way of life as he called it. Perhaps this led to my pursuing other solo sports throughout my life.

As a young girl, I had a friend on my street in Calgary. Marnee Sullivan and I met in Grade 2 and walked to school together. When we were a bit older, ten or so perhaps, her family moved down the street to a house which had a swimming pool in the backyard. In addition to that, her aunt was a swimming teacher, so I became a strong swimmer. I earned my Bronze Medallion in lifesaving before I was scarcely a teenager, I think. This came in handy when I went to Australia in late 1977 on a working holiday visa. The visa was available to members of the Commonwealth on the proviso you arranged your job in Australia only once you got there. I was looking for a teaching job but had arrived during their summer holidays, so I worked as a lifeguard for a few weeks while waiting for the school year to begin.

I also learned synchronized swimming in my friend's pool. This was an appropriate segue from the ballet lessons my mother had me take for about four years as a young child. I accredit that training to my adult love of dancing.

But there is an important adventure missing. It began in mid-1974 after getting my teacher's certificate at the University of Calgary. The reality of finding a job as a teacher of French as a second language in Calgary was unlikely. Instead, I agreed to help out friends going on a six-week canoe trip on the Nahanni River in the North West Territories. The deal was that I would drive their van back to Calgary but only after taking a tour around the Yukon once I had dropped them off at Watson Lake, one of the first towns along the Alaska Highway in Yukon.

First stop was Whitehorse where I presented my qualifications to the Department of Education, and *voilà*, Dawson City needed a French teacher! I even got a chance to check out my new home for the next two years before moving there. I have a funny memory of my preparations back in Calgary. I figured it might be hard to get cheese that far north, so I bought a large quantity, wrapped it in cheese cloth and dipped it in wax! Of course, I discovered on arrival that cheese was most certainly available in the local store!

Not only did I teach French to Grades 4, and 7 through 12, but I was also the English language teacher for some of the junior and senior high students. Robert Service School served children from kindergarten to Grade 12. It was the only school in town, which had a population of 660 during the winter. That number swelled to over 1,000 during the busy summer tourist season.

I had a furnished one-bedroom apartment provided by the territorial government, and it was about a five-minute walk from the school. That was very handy given that the winter temperatures could dip to well below minus 50 Celsius. Fortunately, at those intense temperatures, there was little if any wind. The smoke from the chimneys went straight up. We dressed for warmth, since there were no city fashion statements to make. The hood on the standard parkas was rimmed with fur and provided just a small rectangular window so we could see where we were going.

Light in the winter is at a premium that far north. It was useful to have a flashlight at recess time, 10:30 a.m. The sun scarcely made it over the hilly horizon and by 3:00 in the afternoon it was dusk. I got into the rhythm of hibernation, sleeping almost until noon on the weekends. In the summer it was the reverse. I would easily waken by 5:00 or so.

It was my first teaching assignment, and it wasn't always easy. I learned a four-letter swear word starting with a 'C' from one of the girls in Grade 8 when I had given her an after-school detention. I had not been trained to teach elementary but the little time I spent with the Grade 4 students was quite fun. For that age level I had a fun interactive program called *Voix et Images.* If these young students saw me in the town, they would call out to me, "Bonjour Mademoiselle Christie!" I got quite a kick out of that.

But when I tried to teach drama to the Grade 9 students and direct them so that we could put on a play, I had a real struggle. The play did go on but I didn't consider it much of a success. This played a role in me changing schools. Here's how. An alternative community school in Carcross, Yukon came to our school to put on *The Cherry Orchard* by Anton Chekhov. They did such a good job of staging this difficult play that I was extremely impressed. It seemed it was time to move on and I did at the end of the 1975-76 school year.

Carcross Community Education Centre was sponsored by the Anglican Diocese of Yukon in a former residential school. At that time, I knew very little about that part of Canada's history, which may have been for the better in retrospect. We aimed to be self-sufficient – 60 students from Grades 9 to 12, and 20 *parent members* as we were called. We all lived on site under three rules: 1) no drugs; 2) no alcohol for those under-age, which was 19; and 3) no sex for unmarried members of the community. For the latter, a few of the parent members were married couples.

Students came by choice from across Canada. I taught math, and I was in charge of the kitchen, which meant I was responsible for ensuring that 80 people were fed three times a day! I survived in the latter role for six long months. Oh yes, and we were essentially volunteers; I was paid $75 a month plus room and board were included. I was supposed to stay for two years but I only lasted a year. That was enough. It was one of those character-building experiences for which I have no regrets.

During those three years in the Yukon, I learned new pursuits that I have enjoyed throughout my adult life. New friends *up there* taught me the joys of kayaking, canoe camping, and cross-country skiing under the northern lights. We made wilderness treks to visit characters living off the land in log cabins they had either salvaged or constructed from scratch. One of my teaching colleagues ended up homesteading on an island on the Yukon River, eight miles upriver from Dawson. She and her husband built a log home, raised three children whom she home-schooled, and established a large market garden that is still functional to this day. Yukon summers provide excellent growing conditions!

Again, the theme of place recurs, and the physical environment of the Yukon had me in its spell. I remember feeling overwhelming sensations of love for the beauty of the northern landscapes, and at the same time, recognizing just how hard it was to embrace something so huge. It expanded my heart and nurtured in me a sense of gratitude to soothe my soul.

Two of the later experiences during my time in the Yukon wilderness stay with me to this day. They both took place in 1977, which turned out to be a big year of travel.

The first adventure was a six-day solo kayak trip down the Stewart River to the Yukon River, paddling with the current to Dawson City. I had never attempted such a solo experience before, but I had a few female role models who had shown it was possible.

The very first afternoon out on the river, a black bear swam across the river right in front of my kayak! I was shocked at this immediate first encounter with nature! That evening I set up my tent on the bank of the river. My sleeping bag and mat were ready but as I was cleaning up after supper, I heard the loudest, most primal of noises coming from the bushes behind my tent. It sounded like a large animal in pain or, worse still, one that was angry. I felt I had only one choice, as I couldn't imagine sleeping in this spot.

First, I banged my pots together to make a lot of noise so that whatever animals were back there would know there were other signs of life in the territory. Then I snuck up the bank, stuffed my sleeping bag, folded up my thin sleeping mat, took down the tent, loaded the kayak, and went off across the river to sleep on a sandbar! And this, knowing full well that large animals could swim! I had chosen not to bring a watch on this trip, but I guessed it was about 11:00 p.m. when all this happened, given the light late into the summer evenings.

I don't remember how I slept that night but fortunately no large, angry animal appeared to unsettle me. I carried on the next day. What else could I do? I had no choice but to go on downriver, since to turn back would mean paddling against the strong current. I heard similar noises on the second night but decided not to pull up camp. The third day I saw two fishermen, the first sighting of fellow humankind, and asked what the noises might be. I think they said it was coming from whooping cranes mating! Who knew?

The other memory that stands out was a two-week canoe trip north of the Arctic Circle to Old Crow, a Yukon community accessible only by water or air, or by walking 200 miles through the bush to get there as one of my friends did. I canoed with my friend, Bonnie McLean, who now lives in Victoria. How lovely it is to have someone else I have known for so long, living in Victoria where I have been for over six years now. But Marnee, in whose pool I learned to swim, is still in Victoria and so she takes the prize for longevity in this category!

Back to the canoe trip. In late August/early September we were pushing the envelope on suitable weather for canoe camping, but the fall colours were magnificent. We woke up in the mornings to vestiges of early northern frosts with slivers of ice on the ground. One morning we looked out of the tent and saw many caribou grazing around our campsite! What a special and unexpected moment! That kind of large four-legged animal was most welcome. As for two-legged creatures we did not see any for 13 days. When we finally sighted another human being, he was manipulating a firearm as hunting season was beginning. Needless to say, we didn't pull in to shore to say hello!

It was wonderful to arrive in Old Crow the next day, after 14 days in the wilderness, which was pretty evident when we got the shock of looking in a mirror as part of our welcome back to civilization! How we appreciated the modern convenience of hot running water, flush toilets and comfortable beds! We were pleased with our accomplishment and felt stronger for the experience.

I neglected to mention that at one point we did not know where we were on our topographical maps. We had started on the Eagle River at the small settlement called Eagle, 370 kilometres up the Dempster Highway, well north of the Arctic Circle. The Eagle River flows into the Bell and then into the Porcupine on which Old Crow is located. We were not sure when we were at which river junction, and that was worrying. The reality was we simply needed to go with the flow, literally speaking, to arrive at our destination. It's easy to write that now!

After my forays into outdoor adventures in the Canadian north, it was not a tough decision but instead a natural segue to ride a bike from Vancouver to San Francisco. Why not? I was on my way to Australia after all and thought my plane ticket would be cheaper if I flew from San Francisco instead of Vancouver! A Yukon friend, Greg Caple, then living in Vancouver, helped me buy a 10-speed bicycle there.

I had not had a bike for a long time as it is not a common mode of transportation up north. I read up on how to manage the 10 speeds, learning that the key was to use the ten gears for my legs to go the same speed over hill and dale! My friend taught me how to change a flat tire, as he said I did not deserve to own a bike if I couldn't do that!

I left Vancouver in mid-October 1977. I remember my grandmother, who was 77 at the time, had asked my father if he was going to allow me to do this trip. Apparently, he replied, "What do you expect me to do about it, Mother? She's 27 years old!" And off I went.

I decided I didn't want to cycle due south of Vancouver on the superhighways to Seattle. Instead, I would make my way south of the border by going via Vancouver Island and the Olympic Peninsula in Washington State. This meant I had to take the ferry from Horseshoe Bay in West Vancouver to get to Nanaimo on Vancouver Island. In turn, this decision required that I first had to ride across the Lion's Gate Bridge in Vancouver, a very unnerving experience, to get to the ferry. And then, you guessed it, after arriving in Nanaimo, I rode over the long steep Malahat Pass to Victoria, some 100 kilometres in a day! What a way to start!

My Calgary friend, Marnee, was living in Victoria and welcomed me to her home for a few nights to get over my sore behind! She was astonished I was going to do this long journey solo as she remembered my being frightened in her dark bedroom when we had sleepovers at her house as kids.

Eventually it was time to sally forth from the comfort of my friend's home and I boarded the Coho ferry to Port Angeles. On the way across the Juan de Fuca Strait, I was overwhelmed by the view of the Olympic Mountains and wondered what the heck I was thinking to take on this challenge. Fortunately, Highway 101 goes around these majestic beauties, but in 1977 this was a logging road and there were no paved shoulders for cyclists. To make matters worse, I was not even wearing a helmet, as it was early days for cycle touring and this safety precaution had not yet come onto the market. The good news is I made it without any serious incident and have lived to tell this tale.

It was a lovely ride and it gave me a tremendous sense of accomplishment. I quickly learned that in the autumn the prevailing winds are from the south, which means that they are warm, but it also meant I had a headwind most of the way. It brought to mind the Irish saying, "May the road rise to meet you, and the winds be always at your back!" Well, the last part of that is what a cyclist wishes for but not the first part.

Two particular memories of the trip stay with me to this day and both were related to rainy weather – it was fall on the west coast after all! In the first part of the trip, I don't remember now if it was in Washington or Oregon, I had an especially soggy day and in a small town I stopped at the library for refuge. The woman librarian there was very friendly, and realizing my plight, as camping that night would not have been pleasant, she invited me back to her trailer for a dry night. I was extremely grateful for that hospitable shelter from the inclement weather.

Another time, I was in northern California where Highway #1 turns inland for a while. It was a wet day but I was kitted out in my finest raingear. It is important to remember these were early days in the outdoor equipment field. I had an anorak but I'm quite sure it was not waterproof Gore-Tex. On my helmet-less head I wore a colourful, checked wool scarf, giving me a gypsy-like appearance. On my hands were garden gloves, not quite so gypsy-like. And to top it off, I had plastic bags on my feet over my runners. Needless to say, I was quite a sight to behold but I was managing out in the elements that were less than ideal.

It may have been about midday and the ride was going well enough. I recall coming around a curve that was winding down towards the Pacific Ocean, the first view of it I had seen for a few days. I was elated. Off on the side of the road was a baseball diamond where some young boys were playing. They looked up to see me approaching in all my fashionable glory and one of them called out, "Hey, look at the bag on the bike!" Well, I had to chuckle to myself. In fact, I was pleased they could at least tell that I was a woman!

I arrived safely in San Francisco where I stayed at the family home of a Yukon friend before continuing my journey to Australia. I was fortunate enough not to have a flat tire until the end of my ride, a month and some 1,700 kilometres later! I remember it took me the better part of a day to change that rear tire. It was not fun but I was very glad I didn't have to do it on the road.

By then, I had become rather attached to my bicycle as a mode of transport and was happy to discover I could take it with me on my flight across the

Pacific. I had completed Month One of what would become a two-year circumnavigation of the Pacific, with stops in 15 countries. What a lucky woman I was!

4. En Route Down Under

I **find personal values influence the choices** you make in life. One of mine that has probably stood out so far is my passion for adventure. Other values that go hand in hand are curiosity and the love of learning. I am fortunate to have had lots of energy and enthusiasm to pursue just about anything. Off I went, selecting a variety of places to discover and explore.

I last left you in San Francisco before flying to Australia for a year on a working holiday visa as it is called. The type of air ticket I bought in late 1977 meant I could stop at a number of ports of call en route.

My first stop was Tahiti – imagine going to that South Pacific haven at 27, all by myself! It was my first exposure to a non-Caucasian culture and my first time in the tropics. I thought I had died and gone to heaven. I was able to find an inexpensive and satisfactory place to stay, and since I had my bicycle with me, I had transport. I love to swim and snorkel and found the sea and the coral were beautiful. I learned about tropical rainstorms – there's a deluge and then it's over and, best of all, you may be wet but you are not cold!

I remember cycling to a fresh waterfall, where I was happy to rinse off the exertions of the road. In addition to the island of Tahiti, I visited two of the other islands in French Polynesia, Bora Bora and Moorea. I loved each one and enjoyed the warmth of the islanders who introduced me to such things as the benefits of coconut oil mixed with the perfume of the frangipani flower. It actually worked as a sunscreen, something that quite surprised me. And, oh, how the Tahitians can dance! I was enchanted. How their hips swayed, almost as if to the tropical breezes.

After about three weeks of this self-indulgence, I forced myself to move on. Next was Samoa, both American and Western, in that order. Although it was still lush and tropical, it was already less of a novelty. I was introduced to passion fruit, which I now love, but at the time I thought the name was a joke. A young American woman I had met got together romantically with an Australian man in the small hostel-like place where we were staying, and I thought they had made up the name!

Two other fruits also played a role in my Western Samoa experience. Local men would ask me if I liked bananas, with a sort of *nudge, nudge, wink, wink* look on their faces. I needed no language skills to interpret their message! More usefully, I learned how to eat a mango without too much mess. The children picked them off the ground beneath the mango trees and holding the fruit with the broad end down by their wrists, they created a small hole in the opposite end. Then they gently massaged the fruit so they could suck it out of the hole! What a treat! Mind you, not every Canadian will easily find mangoes ripe and ready for consumption like this!

In American Samoa especially, it was common to encounter men who chose to wear women's clothing and who were remarkably open about their orientation, wearing make-up and jewelry in broad daylight, going about their business and demonstrating all was as it should be. Remember, it was 1977, when in North America this was most unlikely. Another mental souvenir from Samoa was the traditional geometric tattoos. I remember seeing men covered from head to toe with these artistic markings.

Fiji came next, with its British overtones and its mixed population of Indigenous Fijians and South

Asians. My memories of this stop are faint. It is hard to imagine the amazing novelty of the tropics was already wearing off in less than a month!

The last stop before Australia was a brief stay in New Caledonia, a former French territory. I remember feeling unsafe cycling on the roads because of the wild way the people drove. I ended up being interviewed on a local radio station, whether in French or English I don't recall, but the memory that stands out is I was later criticized for speaking in an unflattering way about the way people drove there! Let me just say it was not a place that won my heart.

Then I arrived in Brisbane, Queensland, in late December, when it is exceedingly hot. After cycling about 200 kilometres up the coast, I turned around as I feared my tires might melt into the pavement! I checked to see if I might get a teaching job there but it didn't look hopeful. I carried on, still on the same plane ticket!

In Canberra, Australia's capital city, I stayed with teacher friends from Dawson City, Yukon, Wayne and Kay Jones. Most noteworthy in Canberra were the flies that hovered around your face. They were horrible. Plus, there is no sea in Canberra. I applied for a teaching position but rather half-heartedly and fortunately without result.

Instead, I moved on to the lovely city of Sydney with its magnificent harbour. To my eyes, Australia probably has the most beautiful beaches in the world. I learned at Bondi Beach just north of Sydney about the power of the Australian surf. It both astonished and sobered me, quite an accomplishment really, considering I'm part fish around water. In Sydney I routinely submitted another job application and journeyed on.

Melbourne was my next stop and it ended up becoming my home for a year. It helped that I had some people to visit there – the brother of an Australian man that my mother had met on a plane in Canada! I became a supply teacher of art in a boys' technical school in a town called Werribee, west of Melbourne. It was tough. I had never taught art before and these boys were prepared to make mincemeat of me. Who knew how hard it could be to distribute 20 rulers for an art project? And then there were the differences between Canadian and Australian English. Sometimes the boys would ask for rubbers, which is the Australian equivalent of erasers in Canada. But rubbers in Canada are something else, and not a topic I particularly wanted to go into with young male teenagers!

I remember going home one night after work and looking at myself in the mirror. My face was throbbing from the day's challenges and I asked myself, "Okay, Karen, who's going to win here, you or those boys?" That helped me turn it around. I was eventually asked to teach humanities, which by then I figured meant teaching those young adolescent males to be human! In fact, it was the Down Under version of social studies so there I was teaching Australian history!

In Melbourne I joined a cycling club and met some wonderful people. On one of our best outings, we first took our bikes on the train to get closer to our destination for the day. We then rode to a place for some mud baths! We donned our *cossies* as swimsuits are known Down Under, and jumped into these deep natural mud puddles, for lack of a better name. I will never forget how funny we looked, coated in mud – like original cave people. Then there was a freshwater quarry into which we jumped to get the thick mud coating off our bodies and swimsuits. What fun it was!

After my year in Australia, I went over to New Zealand where I stayed for four months. Initially I traveled there with my mother who had come to spend

Christmas with me in Australia. We drove around the South Island for ten days before she returned to Canada and then I met up with friends from Calgary on the North Island.

Four of us toured in a Datsun 510 sedan for three months. We camped, tramped the tracks as the Kiwis say, sailed in the Bay of Islands, and walked on the 90-mile beach. Again, how lucky was I! We had a ball.

One thing about hiking in New Zealand is that you quickly learn not to worry about getting your feet wet. On a four-day hike (the Heaphy Track) from point A to B, the trail literally disappeared into a slough. It was the morning of the third day so there was no point in turning back because we had already arranged for our car to be at the end of the track. We had no choice but to swim across the body of water that had formed due to heavy rains. My friend Danelle had a fear of water in those days, so the two guys, Matt and his brother, found a way to help her get across. In the process we learned our backpacks would float as they were well lined with black plastic bags. Strangely, I found that out as I went into the water with my pack still on and it pushed my head into the water!

Despite this type of challenge, I loved that visit to New Zealand – well, after all, what was not to like? We were four Calgarians having the time of our lives. Danelle later married her then boyfriend, Matt, and happily we are good friends to this day. I was besotted with Matt's brother, but that didn't work out. Although I was sad about it at the time, it was obviously not meant to be. He married another Calgarian and had a family and a medical practice there. Had that been me, I would not have had the future adventures recounted here.

I returned to Australia after my adventures in New Zealand. Through the Melbourne cycling club, I had met an Australian nurse, Pauline, who traveled with me through the centre of Australia to see Ayers Rock and then north to Darwin. From there we flew to Bali where we cycled for three weeks. It was a wonderful experience, my first in Asia, and what a pleasure it was. I will never forget cycling through vast rice paddies in the early morning mist, passing Balinese along the road as they smiled broadly at these two crazy white women. We saw Bali as few Westerners did at that time. More details follow in Chapter 6.

While working in Australia, I lived in a residence for fourth-year veterinarian students from the University of Victoria (the state of Victoria, Australia, not the city of Victoria where I live now!). I was obviously an outsider, as were some students from various countries in Asia, and so we became friends, an outsiders' club of sorts! This was perfect because it exposed me to more diversity and it worked out that when I traveled back to Canada via Asia, I had people to visit. Stay tuned. More places to be discovered.

5. An Asian Cycling Lesson

The journey that began in Vancouver in October 1977, en route to Australia for a year's working holiday, gradually took on new dimensions. By June 1979, having explored the South Pacific, Australia and New Zealand, I was preparing to return to Canada. However, this was to take another four months or so since I had a plane ticket that allowed me to stop in the capital cities of some countries in Asia – seven to be precise. I still had my bicycle which was considered part of my luggage on flights and it became my wheels once I landed in each new country.

When I describe this adventure, people often ask if I ever encountered difficult circumstances, especially since I was usually travelling alone. Fortunately, they were few. I have chosen to start with this one, just to get it out there, and then I will return to the numerous joys and excitement of the other months.

The most frightening experience was the first excursion on my bike in the Philippines, Asian country number five by that time. It was July, the rainy season, in 1979. On the day in question, I started my solo trip cycling at sea level and had climbed some way toward my destination, the rim of a volcanic crater. There were few villages en route. It was hot so I was wearing shorts. It had been raining a lot but I wasn't cold, given the tropical temperature and my exertions. My shorts were dripping with water.

A jeep came along beside me and slowed down. The driver, who was also alone, opened the window to talk to me as I was cycling along. On the passenger seat, below the open window, I could see a rifle and a handgun. The driver asked me a question I was to hear often in the Philippines, "Where is your companion?" What was I to tell him? That she or he was ahead of me, which was not true and easily verifiable. He knew no one was cycling behind me, having driven from behind. He shadowed me for a while, driving ahead, then slowing down. I felt trapped and could not work out how I was going to get myself out of this uncomfortable situation.

Finally, a hut came into view and there were people in a village-like setting. I stopped and despite not speaking the local language, managed to communicate I needed help. I was welcomed into a humble two-room abode with wide open windows that had no screens. I heard gunshots in the distance. I put my head in my hands and cried, the water dripping off my soaking wet shorts.

Eventually a young schoolgirl arrived. She had been called to help, as she spoke some classroom English. I asked if I could take my bike on the local transport, known as a jeepney. They are jeeps from World War II modified with long seats facing each other at right angles behind the cab. When it arrived, the driver agreed that it would be fine for me and my bicycle to get on board. I can laugh now at my Western expectation that it might not be acceptable. I have since learned that such restrictions in the Western world are often unknown in developing countries where practicalities triumph over regulations. Those were simply my cultural beliefs at play.

As this unnerving event unfolded, I realized that in this culture, a woman travelling alone was considered to be asking for trouble. On my return to Manila, I stored my bike and set off on the bus to explore the country more safely. As soon as I got on board, a Philippine woman asked, "Do you need a travel companion?" I eagerly accepted her offer and was able to continue my travels there in cultural comfort, relatively speaking, and there were no more unpleasant incidents.

When I ask myself what I learned from that experience at the age of 29, the answers are varied. Maybe it is as simple as learning to say yes to life and no to fear. This lesson could be considered a given now in retrospect as I look back at my other life adventures. Perhaps it contributed to my accepting work assignments in places like Ethiopia in the second half of the 1980s, Bosnia in the mid to late 1990s, Kandahar and Kabul, Afghanistan in 2008 and 2011 respectively, and lastly Haiti in 2012 for three years. This is a fairly long story, to be continued!

6. More Cycling in Asia

The **adventures in seven countries** on my way back to Canada provided lots more learning opportunities! Bali, Indonesia was the first port of call. It was a lovely place to start, and I was not alone for those three amazing weeks of discovery, my introduction to South East Asia. The hospitality was lovely, the simple lodgings inexpensive – this was over forty years ago, after all. I learned to bathe outside beside a tank of water with a plastic scoop the size of a small saucepan. Bathing was especially important after cycling in that heat. We needed to take salt tablets to compensate for what we were losing.

The whole adventure is clearly embedded in my mind today. Perhaps most noteworthy in Bali was cycling up to a volcanic lake and then paddling in a dug-out canoe with a local guide to some far-off hot springs. On a par perhaps were the friendly faces, open with surprise at seeing these two foreign tourists on bicycles. At that time, we were novelties. We encountered no obstacles to speak of, unless you consider the roaming rats in our rooms at night! It was only a couple of occasions, but it was definitely the low point of the visit to Bali.

On Pauline's departure to Australia, I carried on solo to Jogjakarta, on the island of Java, to see the wonders there. I managed to take them in, but I developed a nasty fever that lasted for about five days. I didn't know what to do, which was worrying because I was alone. I remember having local massages and fortunately I still had an appetite, which I thought was a good sign. Later, at my next stop in Singapore, I managed to see a Western doctor whose diagnosis was I had most likely had dengue fever. As luck would have it, I've never knowingly suffered any repercussions from the malaise, whatever it was.

Singapore was an odd mix of Western development in an Asian context. Eating was such an adventure that I chose to go to MacDonald's, something I rarely do in Canada. All I really wanted was something familiar. My only other memory of that stop was going to Bugis Street to get a glimpse of the infamous cross-dressers who gathered there. It was quite a trip!

Next on this four-month route back to Canada was Kuala Lumpur, the huge capital of Malaysia. There I was lucky enough to know a Malaysian couple I had met in Australia. They welcomed me into their home, a modest apartment as I recall. A feature there that I still remember was that there was no toilet paper, not even newspaper as we had used in Norway. Instead, there was water to take care of business. That was an adjustment but one that I got more used to as I traveled around.

Malaysia is a culturally mixed society of Muslims, Hindus and Chinese. My host was Muslim and his wife was Hindu of Chinese origin, a unique combination for sure. As a couple they included the three ethnic groups of Malaysia! They kindly took me to Batu Caves outside KL, as the capital is called. The enormous cave is a Hindu shrine, complete with a sacred cow with a fifth leg growing out of its back! I kid you not!

I eventually cycled out of KL to the ancient town of Malacca. It was July and steamy hot. I rode by plantation after plantation of rubber trees, a major industry in Malaysia. Malacca was a small town compared to KL, but it looked like a dirty city, although I will admit that the old Chinese architecture was pleasing to the eye. I was not a short-term tourist with a decent budget so my accommodation options were limited. I chose a small hotel right downtown. My room had a sink, but I had to go to a shared bathroom for a toilet and shower, which I desperately needed!

What a delight it was to turn on the water inside the shower cubicle, similar to a toilet cubicle in a public washroom. Its door ended about a foot above the floor. I savoured the cooling, cleansing powers of the water, and took my time. Imagine my surprise on turning around in the stall at one point, to see a pair of Asian eyes peering up at me! Oh, the indignity of it all! I yelled at the culprit who took flight, having had his fill, I presume, for I had no idea how long he had been there. To add insult to injury, I then had to walk back to my room through a common room full of Asian men. I had no idea which one had been staring at me! Ah well, no actual harm was done.

Hong Kong was next. Although it has similarities to Singapore, it is its own city. It was sprawling, although what was more noticeable was the density of apartment buildings. I stayed in some kind of hostel there, and sadly my maternal grandfather's pocket watch and my wedding ring were both stolen. The only other impression I had of Hong Kong was its phenomenal airport, which, if I am not mistaken, is almost completely surrounded by water. It is quite something to arrive on a runway only to see water on both sides of it.

From there I carried on to the Philippines. I have already described the unnerving incident that took place there when I was cycling. Until then, I thought I was travelling under a lucky star. I still adhere to the philosophy that you get back what you give out. Throughout this journey, I was not afraid and I must have given off that signal. I am taller than a lot of Asians, and no doubt an anomaly to most of those whose paths I crossed. I am grateful that I remained unharmed throughout my journey.

I had some interesting experiences in the Philippines though. In the two short weeks I was there, I noticed that the citizens behaved in a way that was different from what I had encountered to date in South East Asia. They were more open and friendly to me as a Caucasian visitor. Rightly or wrongly, I put this down to their hybrid colonial history with the Spaniards and the Americans. I learned about a couple of customs I found unusual in the culinary sphere. Apparently, dog meat was eaten – a very unsavoury thought to my Western mind. Hard-boiled eggs were popular but not in the way we eat them in the west. The embryo of the egg, that is, the chick, was partially developed! This delicacy was known as *balut* and when inter-city buses made stops en route, vendors would come to the windows of the bus calling out, *"Balut! Balut!"* Needless to say, I didn't try either of these foods.

In the north of the Philippines I was surprised to see pine trees, which I did not expect on a tropical island. Up north in the small town of Bontoc, I encountered indigenous people in their colourful traditional clothing. What I found particularly unusual were the older men, wearing the equivalent of loin cloths on their lower half, topped off by sports jackets to keep them warm in the cooler higher altitudes!

My final memory of the Philippines was of my journey to the airport to leave the country. It was July, the rainy season. The streets of Manila were flooded with rainwater, and who knows whatever else, that was ankle deep and sometimes even higher. I could not figure out how to get myself and my bike to the airport without looking like a drowned rat! I couldn't go in a taxi as I was sure it would not take my bike. I decided to wear my regular cycling clothes, get soaking wet, and change into dry clothes once I was at the airport. When I arrived at the airport, the guard was not about to let in the bedraggled creature before him. He insisted on seeing my plane ticket as well as my passport. Of course, I had both, and was grateful to go into the airport to do my magic changing trick in the washroom.

The next stop on the journey was Korea, where I had another friend from my time at the residence for veterinary students. Remember, this is all pre-internet, never mind cell phones. On arrival at the airport, I went to an information booth to ask how I could contact my friend whose phone number I had. Before sending me off to the telecommunications office in the airport, the employee asked if I would mind if he called a journalist to interview me. I was surprised but I agreed, seeing no reason not to!

I managed to get in touch with my friend and arranged to meet him. First though I had to answer the journalist's questions and get my picture taken, waving hello while straddling my trusty bike! It is a hilarious photo. I'm wearing my Bell helmet, have a huge grin on my face, and I'm waving as if I'm some kind of royalty! I'm wearing a sundress and flip flops, and I'm carrying a wicker basket on my back. The next day there I was in all my glory, featured in the newspaper posted along city walls!

Interestingly, this free publicity came in very handy as I cycled in Korea. I do not speak Korean but all I needed to do was to show the article to those I met to satisfy their curiosity. I found out much later though from a Korean student in Calgary, that the article described me as a 29-year-old spinster! Fortunately, I was not wearing shorts in the photo. At some point I learned, although I don't remember how, that cycling in shorts as I usually was, was like going out in my underwear. Luckily for me I got away with it, without any untoward repercussions.

I had another very special experience in Korea. When I cycled out of Seoul, by chance I met two cyclists who befriended me. They took me back to their town where they fed and housed me for a couple of days. They even took me sightseeing. Then, when it came time to go back to Seoul, one of them cycled with me. We had a big day – over 140 kilometres – and that included having to change a flat tire on my new friend's bike.

When we stopped at a place for refreshments, I got a big surprise. The young woman behind the counter went to get what we'd ordered. When she returned, she was carrying a women's magazine. She opened it up and showed us a full-page photo of my smiling mug! I remember her pointing to me and then to the photo presumably asking if it was me. Honestly, what a fun thrill. I must have asked her to give me the magazine as I have it still.

In Seoul that evening my new cycling friend and I went out for dinner and drank some very potent local hootch. We had to hold each other up as we stumbled back to our two little cube-like rooms that were beside each other. Sometime later when I was back in Canada, I got a letter from this fellow. As I mentioned, I did not speak Korean, nor did he speak English. The letter contained a photo of a young baby, of which I knew nothing, since it had not been possible to share that kind of information. When I showed the picture to my mother, and told her about this adventure, she looked at me sternly and said, "Karen, did you leave him pregnant?"

Japan was my final stop in Asia and before I even got there, I got lucky. The person sitting next to me on the flight from Seoul was a young Japanese man who had just spent six months touring Europe. I mention this last detail because I think it contributed to his deciding to invite me back to his family home in

Fukuoka on the southern island of Kyushu. It was a traditional house, just outside the city. He and his family treated me very well. I slept on a tatami mat and ate meals with them seated on pillows on the floor around a stove that was inset in the floor in front of us. I also remember him taking me to a whisky bar, where glasses of whisky were going for some $50, I think. I was astonished. Overall, I was extremely grateful at being adopted and getting this type of exposure to a country very foreign to me.

From Fukuoka, I cycled south to visit yet another friend from Australia. He and his family lived in Nobeoka. Since he was busy at his job as a veterinarian, he arranged for people to take me out sightseeing. It was such a kind gesture, but sadly I often couldn't understand what I was seeing as the level of English was very basic. I carried on solo to Kyoto, a large city, and Nara, which is nearby and smaller. There I saw deer bowing to receive biscuits – the formality of Japan extends even to its animals!

In Japan, people stared at me but when they realized I knew what they were doing, they would look away. In Korea, they stared, but when I caught them in the act, they would not look away. I found this an interesting difference between these two peoples.

Tokyo was my final destination in Japan and I treated myself to the luxury of the bullet train to get there. The challenge of moving around in Japan for foreigners, or Gaijin as the Japanese call us, is that you cannot read the road signs. It puts you in a position where you are dependent on others. At home in Canada, I am very independent. It was a good lesson to learn that I needed others. I was seldom disappointed with the kindness people bestowed upon me.

My Asian cycling adventures had come to an end. It was a fabulous experience and as it turned out, was pertinent to what was to follow on my return to Canada.

EPISODE III

My 30s in North America
and Africa

7. Teaching in Calgary

From the Far East, I returned to Canada via the lovely tropical island of Maui in Hawaii, a fitting last stop as it brought me full circle in a way. I had started this foreign adventure two years previously on another Pacific island, Tahiti. What an amazing two-year sojourn it had been, with adventures undreamed of. I was full of gratitude for all I had experienced along the way.

I was 29 when I returned to my hometown of Calgary in October 1979. I don't remember now if I had a plan but I was lucky to fit back into North American society easily. At the time, Canada was welcoming refugees from South East Asia. That suited me well. I became part of the receiving infrastructure by becoming a teacher of English as a second language (ESL) in a Calgary junior high school.

In a way, the tables were turned. I felt as if, after months of being a guest in foreign lands, I was now a host to newcomers to Canada. In some ways it was like travelling in the comfort of my hometown, being able to interact with people from other countries in a meaningful way. Such is one of the benefits of Canada. We can travel the world without leaving our shores, thanks to the fact that Canada is a cultural mosaic, a land of immigrants. Another positive aspect of my new life was that it is much more comfortable to teach your mother tongue than to teach a language you have learned at school (French, in my case).

I spent eight and a half happy years as a teacher of ESL at three schools in the Calgary School Board. A contributing factor to that state of wellbeing was that my students, mostly from East Asia, were eager teenagers, who saw education as a privilege rather than a right, unlike some Canadian-born students.

Some of them had come to Canada without their parents and were being cared for by older siblings. I became the proverbial mother hen. In my thirties, I was still considering having children. In fact, if I had had them in my twenties, which was the norm then, I would have had teenagers in my thirties when I was teaching these immigrant adolescents. They responded well to my coddling, making for a pleasant classroom environment.

I can think of a few of my own learning experiences in this multicultural environment of the ESL classes. Having been out of the classroom myself for the previous year as I cycled the western edges of the Pacific, I remember a new lesson that came quickly. Young teenagers can be good mimics and sure enough, one day a four-letter word beginning with 'S' popped out of my mouth. It was immediately repeated by one of my students. Oops! I was annoyed with myself and had to explain my error. As we know, it is often the bad words of a new language that are the easiest to learn!

I have a fond image of a young boy from Sri Lanka. He was 12 and quite mischievous. I once affectionately referred to him as a little monkey. I caught myself on that one, realizing those words might offend from another cultural perspective. Fortunately, I was not called out on this but I did attempt to remove such faux pas from my classroom language.

This same student had a great attitude. I noticed the other kids sometimes called him *Chocolate Man,* no doubt in reference to his dark brown skin. One day, I drew him aside and asked if this was okay with him. He smiled and responded, "No problem! Everyone likes chocolate!" Out of the mouth of babes.

Body language is often interpreted differently in other cultures. In Canada, a wink implies you are making a joke or telling a fib in a playful way. I often did this in my classrooms to see if the students were paying attention or if they understood what I was saying. I had also done this when I taught French. One day in my ESL class, I was going over what various examples of body language might mean. I chose to wink and asked what it meant. An older boy from China did not hesitate to respond, "Sex"! Well, that quickly curbed my tendency to wink in the classroom!

Another memory that bears sharing was an experience with my older teenage students. We had gone to a Chinese restaurant for lunch in Calgary's Chinatown to celebrate Chinese New Year. We sat at a round table with a Lazy Susan on which sat the ever-present teapot. My students asked me if I would like some cold tea. I switched back into teacher mode to let them know that it was called iced tea not cold tea. Well, little did I know it was neither. In fact, it was cold beer, disguised in a teapot because the restaurant didn't have a liquor licence! Ah, the things I had to learn from my students.

Many of us know it is not easy to learn a second language, even in your teens. Still, it helps if you are fully immersed in the new language, although these students went home every day to speak their mother tongue. I came up with an idea, which I like to think helped. I created a school club called Connections. The idea was to connect the Canadian-born students to those who had come to Canada from other countries. We wanted to facilitate one-on-one partnerships to help the newcomers learn more quickly.

We created a club logo, put it on T-shirts and started club activities. I remember taking a school bus of students to Banff in February. I don't know what I was thinking because it was something like 20 below, although it was a sparkling, sunny winter day. I marched 20 students up Tunnel Mountain overlooking the town of Banff. I clucked around them, making sure their hands, feet and noses were not freezing and showing them where to put their hands to warm them up.

The greatest activity for the members of Connections occurred when we all went to visit Expo 86 in Vancouver in March 1986! What a trip that was, seeing pavilions from countries all around the world, along with students from some of those countries.

Late in 1986, after seven years of relative stability in Calgary, I had to take care of my itchy feet. I applied to World University Service of Canada (WUSC) to teach ESL in Indonesia as a volunteer. Instead, I was selected to be WUSC's first teacher in Ethiopia in Africa and, of course, I accepted. I was going to travel to the other side of the globe to connect with other students, just as my students in Calgary had already done.

In December that year I said a sad farewell to my beloved students at Queen Elizabeth Junior/Senior High School. They created a farewell card using the Connections logo to wish me well. I remember one grade nine girl, recently arrived from Hong Kong, looking at me with a puzzled, concerned expression on her face, asking me why I was going to what was to her such a god-forsaken place. She wanted to know whether or not it was my choice to go to Ethiopia. I realized that for her, having arrived in Canada, she was seriously questioning why on earth I wanted to leave it behind and had actually asked for this to happen. It was not easy to explain. I was beginning to recognize I was afraid of getting stuck in a rut. Apparently, I was willing to go to great lengths to avoid such a horror.

Ethiopia brought a new dimension to my international saga, which may not surprise you but sure as heck took me unaware! What a place it turned out to be for me!

8. Teaching in Ethiopia

My **18-month experience** in Ethiopia in 1987-88 changed the course of my life, for the better I like to think. Although I had traveled in developing countries before, I had never lived in one. Nor had I ever been to the African continent. Even though it was just a year and a half of my life, I am surprised some 30 years later just how much and how clearly I remember that rich time.

Being a volunteer with World University Service of Canada (WUSC) is a fabulous experience. The funding is provided through a general service agreement with the Government of Canada. The federal department is now called Global Affairs Canada but until 2013 it was the Canadian International Development Agency, usually known by its acronym, CIDA.

For starters, as a volunteer, you have institutional support through WUSC, which had a field office with Canadian staff in Addis Ababa, the capital of Ethiopia. They arrange for your professional relationship with your Ethiopian host institution. In my case, that was the National Water Resources Commission which Canada had chosen to support, given the world-renowned drought of the mid 1980s in Ethiopia. Canada was the principal funder of the Arba Minch Water Technology Institute (AWTI), a new post-secondary facility some 550 kilometers south of the capital, over the worst roads I had ever seen. It took about ten hours to get there by car although you could fly in much less time, for much more money of course.

Speaking of money, as a volunteer, I received $1,000 a month and in fact that was plenty. My Ethiopian colleagues earned half that. Plus, my furnished on-campus housing was provided free of charge. Mind you, the use of the word furnished is pretty generous. On my arrival, all that was in the one-bedroom duplex was a single bed and a dining table with six chairs. In the kitchen there was a full-sized refrigerator with a freezer component on the top, and a gas stove with an oven. What more could I possibly want, you might ask! Well, in the kitchen aside from the two appliances, a sink and a draining board beside it, there were no cupboards or cabinets. I brought in a small bookshelf and a desk from one of the classrooms to meet those needs. Eventually, I was provided with a comfortable sofa, four armchairs and a coffee table. Compared to the way my Ethiopian colleagues were housed, I was living in the lap of luxury and I shared it with them often.

The town of Arba Minch in the province of Gamu Gofa was what I call the back of beyond. In my mind, I compared it to the Newfoundland of Ethiopia, with no disrespect to our lovely Atlantic province. What distinguished it by Ethiopian standards was that it was at a much lower altitude than the rest of the country. Most Ethiopians are high altitude people. Arba Minch, which means forty springs referring to the incredibly clear water found there, had a very hot and dry climate. Rain was rare and as such, a blessing. I have never felt the same way about rain since my time there, which is probably a good thing, given that I have chosen to live on Canada's west (a.k.a. wet) coast!

Another way to situate Arba Minch is that it is about 200 kilometers north of the border with Kenya in the beautiful Rift Valley. The lakes of Chamo and Abaya were within sight from the hill above the campus of AWTI. Lake Chamo attracted local tourism as it took visitors out in boats to mingle with the hippopotamus and observe from a safe distance what they called the *Azo Gebaya* (Crocodile Market). Enormous crocodiles lazed in the sun along the far shores of the lake. The use of the word market was not to indicate they were for sale but rather that they were hanging out there as vendors do at an outdoor market in a developing country. It is important to note these crocodiles measured up to 20 feet, or roughly six meters, in length.

Lake Abaya, on the other hand, was known for its amazing Nile perch, which apparently weighed up to 200 kilograms. Its succulent and tender white flesh was delicious but unfortunately hard to come by. When you were lucky enough to get some, it often came in big frozen chunks of four kilograms or so. I remember once when the electricity had gone out on campus, I had one of those blocks of the coveted fish in my freezer. By coincidence, I had visitors drop in that day from the Sudan Interior Mission (SIM). When white folks are a visible minority, as is the case in Africa, they often seek out each other. It was a perfect opportunity to cook up all that fish and fortunately my stove was fueled by gas not electricity. I made some variation of a creole sauce, with onions and tomatoes, the two vegetables available. I still remember how good that dish was. The fish tasted like big morsels of lobster meat! I felt as if I had created luxurious lobster Nuremburg! The imagination of a Canadian volunteer in Africa can be an active one!

So, there I am, in the lowest, hottest and driest part of Ethiopia, with not one but two lakes within sight. Perfect! A place to swim! Well, unfortunately not. First of all, I am not inclined to share my swimming space with either hippos or crocodiles, so that ruled out Lake Chamo. Sadly, there is another equally serious reason not to swim in freshwater lakes in many parts of Africa. It is called *schistosomiasis*, also known as snail fever and *bilharzia*, and it is a disease caused by parasitic flatworms. No thank you.

So, to cool down I can tell you my cold-water shower was much appreciated, although I remember in the mornings having to acclimatize to the cold water by putting my head under it first. The heat stored in my head overnight managed to warm the water up just a bit before it cascaded over my body. Let's just say it was an interesting way to wake up. But it was still welcome, given that I didn't have air-conditioning. For that matter, I don't recall having a ceiling fan either. Evening temperatures went down as low as 16 degrees Celsius, but in the daytime, they were well over 30. The fact it was a dry heat certainly helped.

The AWTI campus was still under development when I arrived in January 1987 although the first batch of students had started the previous September. Part of the construction plan of particular interest to me was a 50-metre swimming pool, which naturally would be part of a water technology institute (tongue in cheek of course!). I was sceptical that, despite the school's name, the water in the pool might pose a health risk. Little did I know that I would not have to worry about that at all. Sadly, that was not because they got the water purification process right. No, it was because the pool was not built in the 18 months I was there. I suppose it was understandable but I so wanted to exercise in cool, clean water that I was in denial for a long time. In fact, the reason the pool was not built, so I was told, was the shortage of rebar in the country. That was the first time I learned about rebar and the role it plays in construction. I recognized there were no doubt other building projects that were higher priority than a swimming pool in such an impoverished country.

For example, there were no toilets in the classroom block of the campus. This annoyed me a lot. After all, it was a water technology institute. How could they not have attended to this important feature of an operational campus? Granted, there were more male students and teachers and they could simply relieve themselves outside. I was the only female teacher initially but there were a few female students, whose rights were not being respected, at least not in my mind. Yes, we could each go back to our residences to take care of business. They were not far away, but that was not the point. My neighbour, Hassen, who lived in the other half of my duplex was the assistant dean of the institute. We were on good terms but I could not convince him this should be a priority, even when I threatened to relieve myself in the fountain in the inner court of the administration building to make a point. Of course, I never did, but it was tempting.

This is a good time to mention an Ethiopian proverb I had to keep in mind to help me deal with my impatience with such shortcomings. It goes like this: *Little by little an egg will walk* or in Amharic, *Kes ba kes enkulal beygru yihedahl.* I loved this proverb and still remember the Amharic version of it. I thought if Ethiopia could not teach me patience, I would probably never learn it. It is fair to say that Ethiopia was not very successful in this regard, unfortunately.

I did learn things from Hassen, my Ethiopian neighbour, who eventually came to Vancouver to do his PhD at the University of British Columbia. Hassen is Muslim, which is the case for about 50% of Ethiopians. He was probably the first Muslim I got to know and I learned a lot from him about Islam. It served me well when I was posted to countries with a Muslim majority. In particular, I learned how a Muslim man can have more than one wife. Hassen was a bachelor, about my age. He jokingly suggested it might be hard enough to keep one wife happy, let alone four!

In addition to its low altitude, another feature that made Arba Minch less appealing to most Ethiopians was the fact that it was an ideal climate for malaria-carrying mosquitoes. I took prophylactics and was lucky my body did not react negatively to them. And of course, I was even luckier not to get malaria, which was still possible because the weekly medication is not completely effective. Not all the faculty and students managed to escape the disease. The saddest case was one of our best students, who returned to his hometown of Asmara in Eritrea, which was then part of Ethiopia. It was June and he had gone home for the summer break. While he was there, he developed cerebral malaria and because it was so uncommon at the higher altitudes, there was no medicine available and he died. The existing transportation infrastructure was so weak it was not even possible to get the necessary medicine to him. That really brought home the reality of what it means to live in an under-developed country such as Ethiopia at that time.

Others fortunately coped better. The common perception was if you ate well, your body would be fortified to withstand an illness such as malaria. I found it odd to learn that, upon greeting people and asking how they were, sometimes they would say they were suffering from malaria. It was much the same as here in North America when people who are going about their daily lives mention they have the common cold. It was one of many adjustments.

Along these lines was another reality I found challenging. Eating well was an indication you had adequate resources, that is, you were materially well off. As such, it was a compliment to tell someone they were looking fat. Essentially it was the way to say they were looking well, especially among friends who had not seen each other for a while. The first couple of times it happened to me, I headed over to the storeroom behind the student cafeteria where there was a large scale for weighing sacks of grains and produce. I soon discovered I had not gained weight. My new Ethiopian friends were simply telling me I looked well. It was just another adjustment.

To make sure the scales did not tip in the wrong direction, I instituted a regime of walking up in the hills above the campus. I went in the hour before dusk, as it was a bit cooler then. My Ethiopian colleagues, who were almost all male, expressed concern that it was not safe to go off like that by myself so I invited them to join me, but they always declined. They were academics who had been sent to Arba Minch by their government, not of their own choice. They were grateful to be employed, despite their low salary. On payday, once a month, a small group of colleagues contributed a large percentage of their earnings to a common pot, which would go to a different member of the group each month. I found it an interesting savings plan.

But back to my wanderings. I loved being up in the hills and did not feel vulnerable. I kept my eyes peeled in case there were snakes along the paths but I never encountered any. What I did see were small groups of women out gathering firewood, which they carried on their backs with the help of a rough cord, tied across their bosoms, making me think of a Cross-My-Heart brassiere, popular in North America years ago. We exchanged brief greetings but the women never stopped to chat with the strange *fereng*, the Amharic word for foreigner.

This was not the case on the rare occasions I walked to the town some five kilometers away when I was swarmed by village people calling me fereng. I never got used to all that attention. I longed to walk along and have nobody pay any attention to me. Alas, it was not to be. I remember once being so uncomfortable, I decided to sing as I walked along, hoping they would think I had lost my marbles and would leave me alone. It was not terribly successful. I was close to tears.

Eventually after about nine months on campus, I got my hands on a vehicle through other Canadians working in the region. It was an old white jeep of some kind. It rattled along slowly, making it ideal for visits to the town, not that there was much there – really just one hotel whose restaurant sometimes had what was on the menu. My buggy was anything but airtight and it stirred up copious quantities of dust as we bumped along. My Ethiopian friends called it *Kurtatteh*, which meant something like *Little Wanderer*. In many ways it was perfect. It gave my pals and me a diversion and a chance to do something in our free time, of which there was plenty.

The irony of my 18 months in Ethiopia was I had only 12 hours a week of classes teaching English as a second language and therefore I had oodles of free time but with very little in the way of entertainment. I didn't have a television but then I have never been a big TV fan anyway. This was a long time before the internet. The fax machine was just coming into use. I wrote some 250 letters sent by snail mail during my sojourn there. I am delighted some of my family members saved these missives. They make entertaining reading to say the least.

One accomplishment in the search for entertainment was that I learned to drink beer in Ethiopia! It was partly by default. The options were local soda water, which was actually the healthiest choice but not particularly appealing, and two kinds of pop, which has never been of much interest to me – Pepsi and Orange Fanta. The available wine tasted like very bad Greek retsina. On the Greek theme, there was also ouzo, which I do like, but find it wiser not to drink hard liquor in large quantities. To this day, I love beer, especially in hot weather. My fellow teachers and I would spend hours playing a card game similar to Crazy Eights or Uno, and drinking beer to entertain ourselves. What a simple and innocent diversion!

Only one kind of beer was available. Much later I learned somewhere that a preservative in this beer had perhaps been formaldehyde! Yikes! If this is true, we managed to process it without noticeably unpleasant results. Ethiopians make homemade beer called *tella*. I tried it but can't say it was appealing. They also make mead which is known as *tej*. Now that was more to my liking and I remember an occasion when I traveled with some of my colleagues to a nearby town where we were served this local brew. Oh my, was it powerful! To be handled with extreme care! Good thing I was not the driver that day.

The local honey came from primitive hives made of sticks and found up in the branches of trees. When I asked my Ethiopian neighbour for some honey, he arranged for it to be brought to my home. A man arrived with a big black clay pot with a narrow opening. I was to take some of its sweet contents. We went into the kitchen where I got a big spoon to get it out of the pot. The provider smiled at me and told me a more efficient way was to use my hand so I washed my hand to perform this unusual task. It felt very odd. Then he told me not to put my honey-covered fingers in my hair because my hair would go grey! Luckily, I was not planning to do that. Well, I suppose there must have been some interaction between my hands and my hair as I did start turning grey a few years later!

The other intriguing part of this delivery were the dead bees in the honey. I had to put the golden liquid in a strainer over a pot and set it out in the sun to separate the honey from its creators. What an odd experience for someone who had only ever bought honey in a sealed jar from the supermarket! Ah, the lessons I learned.

How did I feel about being all that way from home, you might well ask. Wasn't it lonely? I suppose there must have been moments when I longed for the relative comfort of home in Canada. I will re-read those letters I sent home to check into that but my memories for the most part are good. I have photos of myself, always with a big smile on my face. The experience was so rich in so many ways that it satisfied my appetite for learning by doing.

My young Ethiopian colleagues, who were almost all male, treated me like a queen, even though I was about ten years older than most of them. One, an Eritrean who had been educated by Catholic nuns, managed to manoeuvre his way into my affections. It started when he offered to help put up the wire mesh I had bought in Addis Ababa to cover my windows in order to keep out mosquitoes and other airborne creatures of the night. The challenge was that the window frames were metal and it was not possible to nail the screens into place. So Menghestab had to pretend he was a carpenter, instead of his actual credentials as a physics teacher, to fit the screens into the windows. They say the way to a man's heart is through his stomach. Well, this was an even easier route to my heart – to protect me from malarial mosquitoes. The buzzing of a mosquito at night in Canada has never bothered me since, because Canadian mosquitoes do not generally carry malaria.

In addition to my Ethiopian colleagues, staff came from several other countries. A German man and his wife from the Caribbean lived across the street but we had no particular rapport. I wonder if perhaps that had anything to do with his dog who howled all hours of the night? Two gardeners came from North Korea, given that Ethiopia was considered a communist state at that time. It was fascinating trying to talk to these two men, as our common language was limited. Several of the other teachers were from India; about seven families as I recall. I learned a lot about them and their culture through our regular interactions. They used to stroll along the road in front of our simple homes in the evenings to socialize. Sometimes they asked me to share a meal with them. I even learned how to make lime pickle from one of them. It was an excellent opportunity to learn about another culture, without even visiting their country.

My other next-door neighbour was a hydraulic engineer from Yugoslavia. He was a great character and I grew to like him a lot. When my youngest brother Tom came to visit me for Christmas after my first year there, he and Martino bonded quickly as my brother reminded him of his own son, whose name was also Thomas. Oddly enough, fast forward to the late 1990s when I was working in Bosnia, I was able to track Martino down in Sarajevo! It was a lovely reunion, although by that time his wife had died and his son Thomas had moved to Toronto. I am sorry to say I did not maintain that newfound reconnection and I suspect Martino may well have died by now. Using the internet, I tried to find his son in Toronto but without success.

Martino had a German shepherd dog, which probably saved his life one evening. He had been out socializing with our German neighbour and was returning home around midnight. His dog greeted him very enthusiastically at the beginning of the path to his house. As the story goes, Martino pushed the dog away but the animal continued to jump up on his chest preventing him from reaching the front door. It was a good thing because there awaiting him, in the dark of night, was a dangerous puff adder.

Fortunately, the effects of the socializing wore off quickly and Martino became very focused. He returned to get his neighbour and with a shovel, I think, they were able to kill the snake. I am pleased to say there was no return of such a deadly creature.

From the town of Arba Minch itself was another international connection. Some Norwegians ran an excellent hospital there. It had the reputation of being one of the best health facilities in the country, which was probably a good thing in case I ever needed medical attention. Their presence was also fortuitous because Solveig, the wife of one of the doctors, came to the campus to help me teach English. What a treat that was to make friends with another white woman in such a remote corner of Africa. It was ironic that her first language was Norwegian, which I had used in my early twenties on the farm in Norway. At that time their language was spoken by only four million people in the world!

In fact, this international mix of personnel on the campus contributed to my eventual decision to leave teaching in Calgary and move to Ottawa so I could work internationally. It seemed as though the whole world was there in Ethiopia. But it was also because it was my first exposure to living as an expatriate in a foreign land. I was a big fish in a little sea. Even the Canadian ambassador to Ethiopia paid attention to me when he came to the south of the country to check on Canada's investment there. He jokingly named me Canada's consular representative in that region. Now that was the kind of attention I did enjoy! At the time I had no idea I would eventually represent the Canadian government overseas, not as an ambassador, but as a diplomat.

But back to other savoury details of my time in Ethiopia – food! I quickly became accustomed to *injera bey wat*, the staple of a spongy, sourdough pancake-like bread with highly seasoned stew, which was eaten with your right hand. Ethiopians are meat eaters, although the 50% who are Orthodox Christians observe 60 days of Lent before Easter by eating only non-animal food. This includes not eating either dairy products or eggs – it was essentially a vegan diet. When Easter arrives, they celebrate by eating big chunks of raw meat!

I have never been a big meat eater, nor have I ever followed a vegan diet. Fortunately, I loved the vegetarian dishes available. One of which I was particularly fond was *shiro*, which is essentially chickpea flour cooked into a gravy-like paste with oil, onions, garlic, and spices, and served with injera. But then I also really liked a very non-vegetarian dish called *kitfo*, which is a spiced form of steak tartar. They always introduced it briefly to the frying pan just to warm it up (*lub-lub*) and perhaps kill any unsavoury morsels residing within! Both are still my favourite dishes when I go to an Ethiopian restaurant in Canada. And I can even order in Amharic ... very important to learn how to feed yourself in the language where you are living!

Since this was my first experience living overseas, I had not realized it's a good idea to bring your favourite recipes with you. This was before the internet so I couldn't find recipes on Google. Instead, I made some up. In particular, since I have a sweet tooth, I baked cookies and loaf cakes, which we used to eat when we were drinking beer and playing cards! My Ethiopian colleagues loved these additions to their diet too – after all, you can reach a man's heart through his stomach as I have said before.

My friends even got to taste a Canadian fruit cake, which my mother had sent me for Christmas. The funny part of that story is that it did not arrive until the following May. Apparently Ethiopian customs could not figure out how to handle it, so I guess they just held on to it. My mother had even splurged and sent it airmail but alas that didn't seem to matter much once it had arrived in the country. Fortunately though, she had liberally dowsed it with rum and wrapped it well so it was just as delicious some six months later! As I remember, it arrived about the same time as some red licorice which had taken almost a year to reach me. Given its preservatives, it was also still fine. My Ethiopian colleagues did not take to it, so I enjoyed most of the package myself!

One last food note: I mentioned my brother Tom came to visit for Christmas. He was on a trip around the world and had arrived in Ethiopia from Nepal and brought some yak cheese with him. It was quite tasty, as cheese was not readily available out in the toolies. Christmas dinner that year was the oddest I will probably ever have: fresh buns that my young housekeeper brought me from the town; bacon, although I have no recollection as to where that came from; and yak cheese! Too bad we had to wait for the Christmas cake!

One of the memories of my brother's visit of four or five weeks was the way he bonded with my Ethiopian colleagues. I especially remember looking out my front door one morning and seeing him standing out on the road hand in hand with one of my favourite male colleagues. It took me aback briefly but I knew it was their way of showing friendship among men.

Speaking of which, another show of friendship was to hand feed close friends. This gesture is called a *gursha*. I never really got used to having an Ethiopian friend gather the stew in a wad of their bread (the injera), and in their fingers want to put it into my mouth! It just did not work for me. You can see how it would be an ultimate sign of friendship. First of all, it meant you really trusted the friend not to put something inedible into your body. Second, it meant the friend would rather feed you than feed themselves. In a country where there had been acute famine, this is saying a lot about your feelings for someone. I remember Menghestab bragging that once when he had attended a wedding, he had not had to feed himself the whole evening! That meant he had many good friends in attendance at the celebrations.

On occasion I had the chance to visit other parts of Ethiopia. One that was particularly important was Awassa, a five-hour drive en route to Addis Ababa. Three Canadian families lived on a compound there. The men worked on Canadian-funded projects through Associated Engineering. I first visited them after being in the country for about four months. It was such a lovely respite from everything Ethiopian, as they had access to familiar foods such as peanut butter and other Canadian delicacies! It was like being home in Canada, at a fraction of the travel time.

Anne and Jack McCracken from Edmonton lived in Addis Ababa where he worked with Hope International. I visited whenever I had a chance. They were perhaps 15 to 20 years older than I was, and I learned that they were church goers. I found it strange I had to come all the way to Ethiopia to meet nice church-going Canadians. I promised myself that on my return to Canada I would try out the United Church.

I had been 'unchurched' since I was in my early teens. I grew up in the Anglican Church where I had loved Sunday school but had found the preparatory classes for confirmation at age 11 to be very upsetting. I would come home in tears, saying to my mother, "I'm not bad but they say I am a sinner and I am not." I went through with the confirmation but that was the end of my time as an Anglican.

Sadly, neither was the United Church the right fit because in 1988 it was debating whether or not it would ordain homosexuals as ministers. I was so offended there was any need for such a debate I was not able to cross the threshold of a United Church, nor did I follow the outcome of the debate. Apparently, the United Church did rule in favour of homosexuals eventually.

Some eight years later in March 1996, I discovered the Unitarians at a new fellowship in the east end of Ottawa where I was living. I knew right away I had come home. This worldwide, faith-based organization, the Unitarian Universalists, has been my spiritual community ever since and it will continue to be where I seek like-minded individuals and guidance in our troubled times.

Apart from Awassa, I was able to travel to Asmara, the capital of Eritrea, which in 1988 was still part of Ethiopia. Menghestab, who grew up there, was my guide. En route, we traveled north of Addis Ababa by land to Bahar Dar and Gondar. From Bahar Dar, we visited Tis Abay, the Blue Nile falls which are the source of that branch of the Nile. In Gondar, we explored the castles of the earlier kings. We then flew to Asmara and from there went all the way to the Red Sea. It was July and I can remember the heat being extremely overwhelming. The Red Sea was shallow and like a bathtub, if not worse. In order to get some sleep at night, the residents pulled their beds out into the streets where it was slightly cooler. I was pretty glad I had not been posted there!

I will end this lengthy chapter by mentioning a trip near the end of my stay in Ethiopia. The town of Arba Minch had Irish Catholic missionaries. I used to go to their residence on occasion and they would feed me something I loved, English custard, but not with their hands of course! There I got to know a lay couple who had adopted an Ethiopian child when she was only nine months old and weighed only as many pounds. By the time I met her, she was about two and a half and she was a healthy chubby child. She loved to eat and I remember learning the word *segebgeb* from her adoptive parents. It is an affectionate word which means greedy, something she could now afford to be because she had come into the hands of loving parents who had the wherewithal to feed her well.

With this small family I traveled to the southwest corner of Ethiopia to the Omo River. As you go further south in Ethiopia, the skin of the inhabitants becomes increasingly darker. The Omo people are very dark skinned. We stayed for a few nights in round grass houses known as *tukuls*. I was sitting outside, looking at a Maclean's magazine that had been sent to me. I had it open to an article about the UK, and there was a photo of Margaret Thatcher. A young Ethiopian child was visiting me. He or she, I don't remember which, looked at the photo and then looked at me, and was clearly asking if that was a photo of me! I was amused. The queen of the AWTI campus had been transposed into the Iron Lady! Perhaps it was time to go home to Canada.

Leaving Ethiopia was emotionally very hard. I remember having just an old-fashioned backpack with all my worldly possessions. It was searched at the airport, while I stood by sobbing. It had been such an intense and broad experience, and I was willingly leaving it all behind. Little did I know what re-entry into my own culture would be like, nor that this was just the beginning of many more foreign adventures in other similarly difficult countries.

As with the aftermath of my experiences in Norway, I continued to be connected to Ethiopians on my return to Canada. I am still in touch with my former colleagues from AWTI. My good friend, Menghestab, now works for the World Food Program. Another friend, Mulugeta, is dean of one of the departments at the university in Bahar Dar in Ethiopia. It was through him that, sadly, I learned of the premature deaths of two of my former colleagues, Paulo and Shibabaw. I corresponded with the latter for quite a long time and sent him US cash whenever I could swing it, as his career trajectory did not take off to quite the same extent as the others. I have Ethiopian friends in Canada and I love going to Ethiopian restaurants whenever I can. Those 18 months in their country had a very strong impact on me in many ways, personally and professionally. Again, I am extremely grateful for this unusual opportunity to learn another perspective on the world.

9. Changing Careers

So **it was that the second half** of my thirties featured a life-changing experience. Looking back, more than three decades later, I realize each decade of my adult life had offered a unique and challenging opportunity. I have already covered the four-continent wanderings of my twenties to Europe, North America, Australia and New Zealand, and Asia. My thirties were about Africa and they prepared me for the decade ahead, my forties.

It was the summer of 1988 when I returned to Calgary from Ethiopia. I was aware I would go through a period of re-entry, of readjusting to my own country and culture. I was fortunate in many ways on my return. For one, I was able to move back into my one-bedroom loft condo which I had rented furnished to a fellow schoolteacher. As I was settling in, I remember going through my walk-in closet with my mother's help. It felt strange to have all that clothing I had not needed for a year and a half.

As I pulled out item after item, I said to my mother, "It's a crime for one person to have all these clothes!"

Her response was, "No, dear. The crime is keeping all those clothes you don't need, when really you have to do just what you are doing – sorting to see what you can pass on to women in need." That motherly advice helped and I have followed it ever since.

There were other times when I felt overwhelmed by all the advantages most Canadians enjoy without question: simple things such as clean running water in our homes; on a bigger scale, our amazing infrastructure, including well-paved roads and controlled intersections, to name just a couple of basics; all the entertainment options available to us; consumer choice in most everything we could ever want – the list is endless. I remember visiting my brother David and his wife who live near the University of British Columbia in Vancouver. Although their home was modest enough at the time, everything in the city seemed meant for all the 'beautiful people'. It was so foreign compared to where I had been living in Africa. I felt as though I no longer belonged in my own culture and country.

Another advantage on re-entry was that I had a job to return to, as a teacher of English as a second language (ESL). The Calgary School Board had given me an 18 month leave of absence. I didn't return to the school I had left, Queen Elizabeth Junior-Senior High School in the northwest of the city. Instead, I was assigned to Clarence Samson Junior High School in the northeast, an area I did not know well. Again though, I was lucky because I got to work alongside another ESL teacher who was wonderful – Rocchina Cafaro. She had a great spirit topped with lots of energy and enthusiasm. It was just what I needed to help me get back into the Canadian swing of things, especially after only 12 hours a week of classes in Ethiopia.

Some of the other teachers did not do as well in comparison to Rocchina. I remember chatting with them in the staff room at the beginning of the school year during preparation time. They were talking about where they had taught the previous year and when it was my turn, they thought I was joking when I said I had been teaching in Ethiopia. Even when they realized it was true, they had little interest in learning more about my overseas experience. Not to worry – I was not there to teach them but the immigrant children, who were mostly from South and South East Asia, and who for the most part saw education as a privilege rather than a right.

One of my fondest memories from that year occurred on March 8th, International Women's Day. I may have learned a little about that day in Ethiopia but it was not noteworthy. In Calgary in 1989 a young adolescent boy from Yugoslavia (it was still a country then) made a lasting impression when he presented me with a red rose! I was delighted and especially impressed that he had not felt self-conscious in making this touching gesture. Little did I know at the time that I would end up spending almost six years in his former homeland.

March 8th became an increasingly important day for me from that time on. One reason is I find International Women's Day to be more inclusive than Mothers' Day. For the latter some women may not be mothers, or perhaps someone's mother has died and the day simply brings back a sad memory. International Women's Day on the other hand is for all women and girls around the world. In some cases, as we celebrate together, we learn about each other, and we may unite in our struggles against the lack of equality between women and men.

Other than that memorable moment, the school year passed uneventfully compared to what was going on in the rest of my life. I was gradually preparing to move to Ottawa, Ontario. As Canada's capital city, it could be seen as the trough for international development, where I now wanted to focus my attention. Although I still loved my students, I no longer had the energy they deserved from a teacher.

I wanted to be more directly involved in world affairs as I had been even in a small way in Ethiopia. I started another letter-writing campaign, but this time to change careers. I worked with a professional to create a new resume, to modernize it, and add my international experience. Although I mailed many letters from Calgary to various individuals and organizations in Ottawa, I did not manage to secure a new job despite my best attempt at networking, which is one of my strengths.

It was scary resigning from a secure job in a place I could call home. In retrospect, I accredit my age at the time – what to me now was a young 39 – to giving me the courage and the faith, I suppose, that I would eventually succeed in a new Canadian setting three provinces away. I carried on preparing to move myself across Canada to a new city and hopefully a new profession.

Gradually things started to fall into place and I felt increasingly assured I was making the right move. For example, a place to live once I arrived in Ottawa materialized. It was a lovely home in an up-market neighbourhood, New Edinburgh. It belonged to my dear friend Linda (Fleming) Krishna whom I had known since Grade 10! She and her husband were going on a sabbatical to France for three months and I would house-sit for them. Perfect!

Then that summer I was invited to Ottawa to participate as a resource person in a pre-departure briefing for WUSC volunteers going overseas, just as I had done two years earlier. I loaded up a large suitcase to leave behind before flying back to Calgary to collect the rest of my belongings.

The next coincidence was one at which I still marvel. On a Saturday evening in late July, I dropped into my mother's house to see if she wanted to go out for Chinese food. As it happened, my mother was not at home; instead, I found family friends who had stopped by on their drive from Vancouver to Wakefield, Quebec, just across the Ottawa River from Ottawa! Heather Best had known me since I was two years old when we were neighbours in Edmonton. She was with two of her four children, moving her worldly goods across the country to the farm she and her husband had recently bought. Her U-Haul was about eight feet longer than she needed for her things, but it was the size of vehicle that met her requirements: seatbelts for her and her two children.

Within 24 hours, I was able to recruit enough friends to help me fill the empty space in the truck with my possessions. Heather would store them in her barn until I arrived in Ottawa and found a place for them! It was a lovely, fortuitous circumstance. What more could I ask for? And so, in August 1989, I loaded what things I still had into my red Toyota Tercel wagon and headed east, still without a job, I might add!

Once in Ottawa, the in-person job search began in earnest. I remember taking an exam to join the public service. I did not succeed. I was disappointed but in retrospect it was in my best interests not to join the Government of Canada at that time because it left the door wide open to all the other wonderful opportunities that came my way.

Despite other negative responses to my inquiries, I did eventually start work within five weeks of arriving in town, at World University Service of Canada (WUSC) with whom I had served in Ethiopia. Three months later I moved into a charming duplex, also in New Edinburgh where I had been house-sitting. My new home was bigger than I needed but I got it at a reasonable rent because the owner was working overseas with WUSC and she thought I was a secure bet!

It was a nice full circle, one that launched me on the next 27 years of my career. I was now a senior program officer managing education and training programs for a non-governmental organization. It was a good fit and I was very grateful!

EPISODE IV

My 40s in North & South America and Europe

10. Working with NGOs in Ottawa

From 1989 to 1996 I worked in Ottawa with two non-profit, non-governmental organizations (NGOs), implementing international development projects, mostly in the Americas. I really liked the work, even if initially it meant a 25% salary reduction from teaching in Alberta. I was now managing projects funded by Canadian taxpayer contributions so the money needed to be spent wisely. I became a steward of Canada's public purse, albeit through an intermediary, the NGOs accountable to the Government of Canada.

Having been a teacher for 13 years, I was well suited to work on the Canada Training Awards Project, CTAP, at World University Service of Canada (WUSC). The project was funded by the federal government through the Canadian International Development Agency (CIDA), and WUSC was sub-contracted to a private sector firm, ARA Consultants in Toronto. Together we were the implementing partners of the project. Mid-career professionals in the Leeward and Windward Islands were selected by their governments to come to Canada to study in our post-secondary institutions. Through the vast WUSC network, we placed these individuals at the appropriate colleges or universities and then mentored them during their sojourns in Canada.

I was responsible for supporting the students in Ottawa and institutions in the east. Some were stationed in Montreal but not elsewhere in Quebec because French was not spoken in the part of the Caribbean of our beneficiaries. I also traveled to New Brunswick and Nova Scotia to visit them and ensure all was going according to plan; as well, we followed up from Ottawa. I remember learning to ask how much their long-distance phone bills were as an indicator of how homesick they might be. I can recall a student in Montreal who explained how odd it was for her to hear a winter weather forecast of sunny and cold. For her that first word just did not go with the second! The same student explained how difficult it was to walk on the icy streets of Montreal. She told me she couldn't walk with her hands in her pockets, even though that would have kept them warm, because she needed them free to give her extra balance and manage her footing on the ice!

Gradually I took on more projects in other countries of the Americas. I helped support colleagues on a project in Costa Rica partly because I spoke some Spanish, thanks to a five-week immersion course in Costa Rica in 1985. Next, WUSC was the organization selected to launch two other CIDA-funded projects starting up in Argentina and Uruguay. This initiative came about as a result of a visit by the then-Minister of External Affairs, Joe Clark, who promised to support the human resource development of these two countries, although they were not common recipients of development aid. The project sectors in Uruguay were computer science and the processing of ready-to-eat meals; in Argentina, they were forestry, marine science and geology.

I participated in the original inception mission for these two projects in March 1990. What an intriguing experience that was, and it really put my Spanish to work! I then had to summarize it in English in an inception mission report, which would later form the basis of a project implementation plan. These are components of the international project management cycle.

I was fortunate to have been so involved in these two projects because in December 1990 WUSC went into receivership! I had been the last officer-level employee hired some 16 months previously so I thought I would be the first to go. As luck would have it, I was not. As the saying goes, necessity is the mother of invention and off I went to ARA, who knew me from CTAP, to market my worth and help them get engaged in these two new projects valued at one million dollars each. It worked, but not in the way I expected. WUSC had recognized my value vis-à-vis these projects and asked me to stay with the organization under the receivers, Ernst and Young. *Que suerte*, as they say in Spanish – what luck!

WUSC continued to be a good experience for me. I ended up travelling twice a year to Argentina and Uruguay over a three-year period. That was indeed a treat. They were probably the two most developed countries I was to work in! I remember too that the Argentinian project became my foray into what was then called 'women in development'. This term morphed over the years to eventually be called 'equality between women and men' in the mid-2010s.

As in all good international development projects, we worked with institutional partners from the host countries. We met first with the umbrella counterpart and then the sectoral ones, before finishing with all the partners in a plenary following a week or so of meetings. We dealt with the project components and then it was my turn to introduce CIDA's cross-cutting themes of sustainability and gender equality.

In my intermediate-level Spanish, I presented Canada's requirement for both women and men to benefit from the project. I still recall the look on the big burly Latin forester as he gradually grasped what I was saying. Recognition of the issues crept across the faces of all around the table. It was something with which everyone was familiar. Women and men learn to co-exist out of necessity in their homes but they were a little surprised to have the topic brought into the workplace. In many ways, it added levity to the discussions. People smiled in awareness of the challenges for all societies to benefit from the contribution of both genders.

As with many of WUSC's projects, the ones with Uruguay and Argentina involved project participants coming to Canada for practical attachments. These were like co-op assignments minus a salary although their expenses were covered without any expectation that the trainees would join the employer at some point in the future. In fact, it was quite the opposite as trainees were expected to return to their home countries to share their newly gained skills to strengthen their sector back home. Two trainees from Argentina had a very unusual welcome to Canada. As they say, some real-life events described would never be believed in fiction. This is one such scenario.

I had gone to the airport to meet the two mid-career Argentinian men who were arriving for practical attachments in marine science in Canada. In my role as a senior program officer, I was to welcome them and make sure they were comfortably set up for their sojourn in Canada. One aspect of that was financial so I asked if they needed some Canadian currency. They did so we walked over to a branch of the CIBC on Bank Street in downtown Ottawa. Well, while we were there, an armed bank robbery took place! Yes, that's right! It was hard to believe but there we were, down on the floor as requested and leaning against the counters. Can you imagine a worse welcome to Canada? Few Canadians have ever had this horrible experience in a whole lifetime.

Anyway, one of the men beside me whispered very quietly that he had about two thousand US dollars on him, and had worked very hard to pull together that amount. I tried to assure him his money would be safe. Fortunately, it was, and no one was hurt. After the armed bandit fled the scene, the bank staff calmly requested that everyone remain on the premises. The police were called and we all had to give a written statement about what we had witnessed. Now this was another challenge for my guests, as English was not their first language. In the end we all managed and it was intriguing to realize everyone had seen a different aspect of the robbery. I don't recall now what I did after we left the bank to assure my guests that they would be safe in Canada. But seriously, their visit could only get better after that traumatic introduction to our fair land.

NGOs in Canada are often the backbone of international development since they are a fraction of the size of the government funders, who are not nimble enough to implement projects. NGOs also have substantial expertise and experience. Sometimes these characteristics add to their appeal as partners for the private sector. It is an interesting mix of orientations. I have always been attracted to the benefits of a team approach where each entity offers its strengths, creating a more solid whole.

In the mid-1990s in Ottawa, donor dollars were decreasing. NGOs generally work hard to diversify their funding to avoid being dependent on one donor, should that well dry up. At WUSC a few of my colleagues had already moved on, mostly to other NGOs such as CARE Canada and the Association of Canadian Community Colleges (ACCC) – pardon the alphabet soup here! (Were we perhaps military wannabes?!)

After four years at WUSC, I eventually followed suit, replacing a woman going on maternity leave from ACCC. As its name implies, it was also in the field of education and training. I joined the Americas team on the international side of the house. Again, I worked on another scholarship program funded by Canada but this time with countries from CARICOM, which stands for the Caribbean Community. This time, too, the NGO where I worked (ACCC) was sub-contracted to the private sector, Universalia Management Group in Montreal. The work was very similar to what I had done at WUSC.

At ACCC, I was successful in moving up to management although it was relatively short-lived as Government of Canada funds were shrinking by 1996. Nevertheless, in the fall of 1995, I led an ACCC fact-finding mission to northern Chile to determine the feasibility of a training program to develop technical expertise in the mining sector. That was a fairly challenging undertaking in a uniquely harsh environment, the Atacama Desert.

Although I wrote the subsequent project proposal, I can't remember whether or not it was actually funded. No doubt this is related to the fact I decided to step away from ACCC in May 1996 after three years there. It felt a bit strange to do this but I was looking forward to a new experience that I had organized: to volunteer as a host at Canada Olympic House in Atlanta for the summer games. I thought it might be time to change focus and maybe that would be in the world of international sport. I knew I wanted to continue in the international domain but possibly in a new genre.

Being in Atlanta for the games was an eye-opening experience. The Canadian Olympic Association put on a comprehensive pre-departure briefing for its volunteers and off I went into the seductive southern culture of the USA. Again, luck shone upon me and I made a connection to a gracious southern family. Laurie Miller, who was about my age, and her mother of 71, which even at 46 seemed quite old, welcomed me into their southern home. Laurie was an architect, and her mother had decided she would help out in one of the cafeterias at the Olympic Village. I was impressed by her energetic spirit. Now that I am the same age, I can relate!

Their home was a comfortable townhouse and by the time the games had begun, every spare level surface had become a bed for others involved in putting on the games. We were quite a diverse little family. There was even a swimming pool in the complex. I can tell you I was very grateful for that liquid cool-down at the end of a long, hot shift in downtown Atlanta in July!

We worked hard at Canada Olympic House, infected with the spirit of the games and Canada's role in them. It was a pleasure to welcome the families of our athletes to their home away from home. However, I did learn through this experience that the sports world, even if it was international, was not for me. What next?

11. Shifting Gears to a Multilateral Organization

In Ottawa after my month-long visit to Atlanta, Georgia, in mid-August 1996, I met up with one of my former WUSC colleagues, Marianne Wightman. Working together for four years we had become friends, not to mention that we looked similar and would on occasion be mistaken for one another. Over lunch, I learned she had been trying to contact me as she had an assignment for me.

Marianne was WUSC's representative for the United Nations Volunteer Program which was recruiting Canadians to participate in the international supervision of the first elections in post-conflict Bosnia and Hercegovina (BiH), hereafter called Bosnia for simplicity. She was contacting volunteers from the WUSC data base of Canadians who had previously been posted as part of its general volunteer program, under which I had been in Ethiopia. Fortunately, I was able to turn myself around in about a week and by late August, I was on my way with several others to Bosnia via Vienna, where we awaited the signal to proceed to Sarajevo.

At that time, I did not realize this first foray to the former Yugoslavia was to occupy me there for the next six years – the last four of my forties, and the first two of my fifties. It was another great fit, although I would never have guessed it would be the case. For starters, I had always been apolitical, which was useful when getting involved in the elections of another country. One of the best attributes in this line of work is impartiality. Furthermore, I had not followed the news about the Bosnian conflict. I simply could not – it was too horrifying. I believe this was an advantage because it helped me to be more neutral.

I soon discovered the administration of elections is a logical and methodical process, which suited me to a T as I had a concrete, sequential way of learning and doing things. Still, as a child, I had never dreamed of working in election administration in a post-conflict environment when I grew up!

The first experience of being an election supervisor in Bihac in Bosnia opened up a fascinating new world. The General Framework Agreement for Peace (often known as the Dayton Agreement since it was signed in Dayton, Ohio in December 1995) had identified the Organization for Security and Cooperation in Europe (OSCE) as the body that would oversee the implementation of the peace agreement. The OSCE Mission to BiH had four departments: stabilization (i.e., security), human rights, democratization and elections. The OSCE has 57 member states from Europe, Asia and North America. Its origins date back to the early 1970s when it was the Conference on Security and Co-operation in Europe (CSCE), created to serve as a multilateral forum for dialogue and negotiation between East and West.

In Bosnia's post-conflict environment in August 1996, it was agreed among the OSCE member states and the host country that, in addition to the local election authorities, there was a need for international election supervisors as well as international election observers. The difference between the two is what the names imply: the former is hands on, while the latter simply observes. We were the former, election supervisors. We were briefed and trained in how the elections were to be run. We worked in pairs under the leadership of other internationals who were working as an elections officer, a trainer and a core supervisor whose job was to find accommodation, drivers and cars, as well as interpreters for all the supervisors.

But first we had to get to the country! The journey to our places of supervision in Bosnia developed into quite a story in itself. On arrival in the shell of an airport in Sarajevo, we waited for six hours or more, not knowing what our final destinations in Bosnia would be. The airport lacked any facilities to speak of and was not yet open to commercial traffic, due to the heavy bombardment that had taken place there. The presence of a plane full of foreigners apparently provoked a logistical nightmare for the OSCE organizers. As I recall, we may have been given bananas to sustain us as we waited and waited. Finally, as night fell, they started to mobilize us.

I was part of a group transported in a mid-sized bus that could have been a school bus under normal circumstances. Let's just say it was not a particularly comfortable ride and it was exceedingly long. At one point, we stopped in the darkness at the side of the road for those who needed to relieve themselves. Well, first of all, we were not allowed to go off the road into the bushes because of the threat of landmines. But never mind that significant detail, it was also pitch black! Not only that, but armed guards were travelling with us and even though they stood with their backs to us, it was not easy to relax enough to take care of business. The only thing that helped was knowing the alternative was no more attractive, getting back on the bus and bouncing along with full bladders for who knew how long.

After at least six hours of travel, sometime after midnight we arrived at what was called the Metal Factory in Banja Luka in the Serbian Republic of BiH. This military base was so named because that is what it had been before the conflict. It had since been taken over by the British contingent of the Implementation Forces, otherwise known as IFOR, to house their security operations. It was wonderful to have finally arrived somewhere, even if our individual destinations the following day were still unknown. Even better was the hot cup of English tea with milk and biscuits. A cup of tea has never tasted so good! We slept that night on military cots under a high warehouse ceiling, grateful to be safe and cared for.

In the morning, we were separated and sent to our various destinations. It is interesting that I no longer remember how I traveled that last lap of the journey to Bihac. It was only a couple of hours I think but we had to cross the Inter-Entity Boundary Line (IEBL) between the Serbian Republic and the Federation of BiH. It had been the former front line of the conflict but now it was what the name implied, a boundary. It was intentionally not named a border because the two entities are one country, not two separate ones. However, in those first years after the peace agreement was signed, it was not particularly easy for anyone to move from one entity to the other. It was even difficult to make a phone call from one to the other. It seemed outrageous that such basic communications were not possible as it compounded the angst of those who were internally displaced and unable to contact family and friends on the other side of the boundary line.

Once in the town of Bihac (my destination) in the BiH Federation, I remember my feelings of gratitude on seeing military tanks manned by international forces as they manoeuvred down the streets. In this part of the Federation, they were usually Canadian troops since each contributing nation had been assigned responsibility for certain areas. For those who have worked with NGOs, their view of the military is seldom positive but I quickly learned that in a relatively new post-conflict environment, troops have an important role to play. NGOs do not often work with the military and so do not generally have firsthand experience of military strengths and what they offer in situations where their presence is needed. I quickly learned that the term 'military intelligence' is not an oxymoron.

On arrival in Bihac, I was assigned my accommodation, which was at the home of my 19-year-old Bosnian interpreter, Dinko, his sister and his parents. My supervisor partner, a woman from Egypt, was lodged with another family. Our driver was also a young man from Bihac. I will always remember the orientation given by these two young men to the international half of our team of four. It was a visit to the cemetery. Bihac had been under siege for several months during the conflict and there were many fresh graves in the town.

I was received most graciously by my new hosts, who were no doubt both anxious and hopeful about the arrival of international election supervisors. Our presence signified the potential for the country to move forward after the harsh realities of the conflict when neighbours who had previously co-existed in peace, were suddenly pitted against each other. On a more micro level, the OSCE mission meant employment and opportunity for many Bosnians who had coped with austerity throughout the long conflict. At only 19 years of age, my interpreter was bringing much-needed financial resources into his family, not to mention he became the family spokesperson, given his knowledge of English.

I remember at least two hilarious conversations that were the result of limited language capacity on my part. They were simple domestic situations but they had us laughing out loud. One was related to my asking what meat was in the delicious stew I had been served. I am not sure exactly why but Dinko said it was rat! I am also not sure if he simply could not find the right word or if he was joking, because of course it was not rat meat in the stew. His mother was understandably horrified when Dinko explained the communication error that caused so much laughter.

The other linguistic incident took place when Dinko was not present and I tried using my little Bosnian phrase book to get something across. I can't remember the details now but it involved Coca Cola and the local word for rooster! They were similar and caused much confusion, followed by peals of laughter when Dinko finally came home and tried to explain the miscommunication. This is partly why I have always loved learning another language in person: it reduces an adult to the linguistic capacity of a toddler and often the best way to deal with it is through laughter.

We had left Canada for this assignment in late August 1996. The election was on September 14th, which gave us over two weeks for our travel and orientation. We felt we were well prepared to take on the task of supervising the elections, which were the first to take place since the peace agreement had been signed just nine months earlier.

We rose early on election day and our little team of four headed out well in advance of the polls opening at 7:00 a.m. We had been assigned to supervise six polling stations located just outside Bihac and all the way out to the IEBL, the former front line. It was going to be a long day and we were expected to remain on the job until all six of our polling stations had closed and the votes cast in each of them had been counted.

We all experienced a certain level of anxiety. Mine came to a head in the morning in a polling station near the IEBL, in a town that had been heavily damaged in the fighting. Among the non-sensitive election materials was a large, sealed manila envelope. I am not sure why but before even opening it, I became anxious about a shape I could feel inside the envelope. It felt like two hard cylinders at right angles to each other. For some reason, I thought it might be a handgun! Nobody could confirm what it was and I was too worried to let anyone even open the envelope. So, rightly or wrongly, I carried the sealed envelope outside and sought out a local police officer. How Canadian, eh, to trust a man in uniform?! Fortunately, my fears were groundless. On opening the envelope, I discovered the suspicious objects were two good-sized candles that could stand on their own should the electricity go out that evening! What a relief, for sure, but I felt embarrassed I had been so paranoid. It clearly indicated my level of stress.

The rest of the day went relatively well as I recall but it went on for about 24 long hours. We were starving by the time we had finished even though we had taken snacks with us. In post-conflict Bosnia, the restaurant business was not exactly up and running yet!

The international supervisors remained in place for the next few days after the elections in case we were needed to follow up any irregularities. We debriefed and wrote reports on the proceedings of the election day. We also made time for some fun. I remember a fancy-dress party organized by all the international players. I managed to dress myself up as Lady Diana! I had brought a grey synthetic knit suit with a faux brocade pattern on it. As well, I had a hat with a very wide brim, the kind that Lady Di might have worn. To top it off, my interpreter's sister lent me a pair of platform pumps! I even took off my watch, which was quite distinctive, to hide my true identity. Sunglasses added to the deception. We had a good time that evening, finding it a great opportunity to let off a little steam after the tensions of the whole exercise.

I loved the ambiance of the three-week experience in Bosnia, my first of six assignments there. It was just what I'd had in mind when I made the decision some eight years previously to work internationally. The diverse mix of people, professions and nationalities was what I had pictured when I left my teaching career of 13 years.

12. Assignment #2 in Bosnia

I **didn't return to Bosnia until** the following year when I had the opportunity to be a voter registration supervisor with the OSCE for ten weeks in the spring of 1997. Again, I was sent to a small town that had suffered a lot during the conflict. Maglaj was a predominantly Bosniak[1] area in the Federation of Bosnia and Hercegovina, also not far from the former front line and, like Bihac, it too had been under siege for a long time.

I was lodged in the home of a couple about my age (late forties). Their two children in their twenties were now living in Germany. In fact, they had left Bosnia during the conflict. We learned the parents used to walk for hours over the mountainous countryside to make phone calls to them. The absence of the children was obviously still painful for their parents, especially their mother, even though the peace agreement had been in place by then for over a year and a half.

I like to think that having international guests was helpful for them not only financially but also perhaps to distract them from the hardships they continued to endure. One of the local OSCE staff was billeted there too, a young woman working with us as an interpreter, and also a fellow supervisor, a British woman in her thirties. I remember her name was Vicky and she was a former captain in the British military, not an insignificant accomplishment.

We were well looked after as our meals were prepared for us by the woman of the house. However, life was still difficult given that we had electricity only six hours a day, three hours in the morning and three in the evening. It affected the availability of running

---

[1] The term Bosniak refers to Bosnians who are Muslims.

water, something we take for granted in North America.

Vicky and I usually ate our meals in the presence of our host. Often though the local interpreter was not with us, and so we had our heads in the phrase book trying to communicate. As usual, it suited me to be learning another language which resulted in lots of laughter as we were just like children trying to express ourselves.

Supervising the voter registration process was actually quite fascinating and being in one place for ten weeks instead of just three gave me more time to understand the context better. I can't remember how many hours a week we spent in the voter registration centres but I do recall it was like a regular work week. Again, we had a driver to get us there daily and of course, we still needed to work through an interpreter. We also had time to get to know the local staff of the centres, being with them for hours on end.

The job was to create new voter lists for the next round of elections. Citizens were to visit the registration centres with an official piece of identification to ensure they would be eligible to vote. Given that some people had been displaced by the conflict and recognizing that some of them no longer had any valid identification, this was not a straightforward task. The role of the internationals was to ensure all citizens were treated fairly and given adequate assistance in replacing their documentation, no matter what their ethnicity.

I remember hearing the stories of loss from the conflict. The chairperson of our centre was a young woman who had lost her brother, which was having a long-standing impact on her family. Oddly enough, I had an interesting language learning experience through this woman, whose name I remember as Alma Muratovic. For some reason she often had swollen fingers, which she did not like. However, she was able to poke fun at herself by calling her fingers *kifle*, which was a small croissant. That is what her fingers looked like to her: little puffed Pillsbury dough boys.

I made some good international friends during that assignment, mostly from Canada and the US; I stayed in touch with an American woman for some 20 years afterwards. I visited her one summer in Massachusetts and we later overlapped in Afghanistan. The 'elections circuit' as we called it, attracts a particular sort of personality, not dissimilar from mine, I suppose. We were educated, sometimes at loose ends and we sought intriguing, meaningful adventures, which we got in spades.

The assignments could be either short or long term. The former is usually less than two weeks and can be compared to camp for adults! We are called to a foreign destination, usually in a place where we would not necessarily go on our own, and our lives are regimented by others like us, who are on the long-term assignments. They welcome us, brief us, and assign us to various parts of the country where others receive and orient us, providing accommodation and local staff (drivers and interpreters) who make it possible for us to do our job.

The monetary compensation usually just covers our expenses but that is better than camp or a place like Club Med, where we have to pay for the experience. That is part of the hook. We are immersed in another cultural and political context and we learn so much at no financial cost to ourselves. It allowed me to continue to learn by doing. That being said, I would not have dreamt I would end up having such intense and memorable experiences in a post-conflict environment. If anyone asked me to describe my ideal job, I would never in a million years come up with the job description: international election supervisor in post-conflict Bosnia!

But back to the voter registration process in Maglaj in Bosnia. For the first time in my life, I encountered adult illiteracy. To be frank, I was stunned. As a former teacher, I found it incomprehensible that an adult in Europe was not even able to sign their name. As a North American, I was used to pre-school children who could print a legible version of their name. It was an eye-opener to learn this was not always the case in Bosnia.

I also had my first experience verifying the identity of a woman dressed in an *abaya* and *niqab*. This was necessary so the staff at the voter registration centre could legitimately register her to vote. It turned out to be relatively simple, compared to how it can be politicized here in Canada. The women staff of the centre would take her aside to where there was enough privacy for her to show that her face matched her identification card. That is not to say it did not cause a bit of a stir. Most Bosniak women (Muslims) did not choose to cover themselves in black from head to toe. To my understanding, there were just a few women who made this choice at that time, the second half of the 1990s.

As I mentioned, ten weeks was long enough in such an intense setting to form some strong relationships with people, both local and international. As the end of our stay approached, I remember feeling the stress of the assignment coming to an end. It was amplified by ongoing security concerns with regard to us being transported safely back to the regional centre in Zenica, where the international staff responsible for our well-being in the country were located. It resulted in uncertainty about when we would actually leave Maglaj. In the end, we had less than 12 hours' notice about our actual departure time. I was physically and emotionally exhausted as we pulled out of town with our local driver who also acted as our interpreter. I have a very sad memory of sitting alone in the back seat of the car with the tears streaming down my face as we pulled out of town, past the many destroyed, deserted and bullet-ridden houses along the roadside. This perpetual theme of departures was a low point. Little did I know at the time how much more intense they would get.

13. Assignments in the Serbian Republic

Following the voter registration assignment in Maglaj, I hadn't been in Ottawa for long before I got a request from the OSCE to return to Bosnia. This time both my role and my destination were identified in advance. I was to be an international trainer of the election supervisors for the next elections and I would work out of the OSCE Regional Centre in Banja Luka in the Serbian Republic of Bosnia and Hercegovina. This was the same place where I had slept that first night in Bosnia a year previously. Again, it was a good fit: after all, I had been a teacher for 13 years.

For this assignment, my third in the country, I lived in a furnished apartment on my own. It was pleasant enough but quite a switch from the experience in Maglaj where I always had company and where I was fed three meals a day. However, I adjusted, as one does. I remember getting to know the local driver who picked me up every day to take me to the office and bring me home in the evening. We were a similar age (late forties), whereas previous drivers I had met were younger. He was grateful to have the employment to support his family. It was he who told me the news in late August 1997 that Princess Diana had been killed in a car accident in France. Many of us will remember where we were when we got that shocking news. It was surreal to learn about it in a country torn apart by conflict. And sadly, it was not to be the last time in former Yugoslavia to hear of devastating world news since I ended up working there until the end of 2002.

This being my third time in Bosnia, I was becoming more and more familiar with the various roles all the international participants were playing. I was leaving behind my hands-on supervisory role, first of the elections themselves and then of the voter registration process, to take on the task of training incoming election supervisors. I had moved quite naturally into the long-term roles although this assignment was only for a few weeks. My colleagues were other trainers, both local and international, and we worked together to come up with a procedural manual for the short-term election supervisors.

Then there were the international core supervisors who, as I have mentioned previously, prepared for the arrival of the supervisors by recruiting local drivers and interpreters, and arranging for their short-term accommodation. As well, there were international election officers who liaised with the local officials responsible for holding the elections. I held the former in awe. Little did I know that my next assignment would be that same position, international election officer!

This month as an international trainer in August and September 1997 passed relatively smoothly, not to say that there were no tough times. There were for sure. The long days at the office were intense but we delivered the results. The elections took place as planned in September and we all survived intact.

I don't remember now whether or not I returned to Canada before my fourth assignment took place. I was posted again in the Serbian Republic but this time in the smaller town of Prnjavor, just north of Banja Luka. Now I was going to be an international election officer, the position I had previously held in such high esteem. Either I had done something right as an international trainer or no one else wanted to be the election officer and head of office in Prnjavor. Perhaps both of these factors were at play. Still, I was keen to take on the new role – learning by doing again!

As usual, I jumped right in although not without some reflection about whether or not I was suitable material for a more political role. I had always considered myself apolitical and in reality, I felt it was a bonus in the work I was doing. As foreigners, we didn't have the same baggage, as it were, as the local authorities. We had not lived through the conflict. We didn't have the same preconceived notions about ethnic groups. In fact, as I noted before, I had not followed the Bosnian conflict while it was happening. I could not bear to. It was easier to take people at face value, once there, on the ground. Neutrality is an important trait to bring to the table in a post-conflict environment. I felt I had it in spades.

As it turned out, the role of election officer suited me well as it was a broader, more comprehensive job and I was continually learning, as my range of interlocutors expanded. I thrived on the opportunities to interact more regularly with local officials. Plus, I managed my multinational team relatively well. I qualify that because there was one individual from Eastern Europe, Bulgaria as I remember, who did not take kindly to having a woman as his boss. We duked it out. I prevailed, but not without some effort. I found solace through one of my housemates who was from Spain and who had some wonderful Spanish food delicacies which he shared generously. Sometimes that's all you need – simple pleasures.

It is interesting what memories remain. For example, did the election for which we were preparing actually take place or was it postponed? I'm quite sure it was postponed. Although it was a good experience, I was not unhappy when the month came to an end. It was starting to get cold in Bosnia in late October/early November and our housing did not have central heating. It was time to return to the comforts of home in Canada. I was sharing my two-bedroom home in

Ottawa with a friend all this time so I had a home to return to and for that I was grateful. There were no big, emotional farewells after this assignment. But not to worry – there would be more.

14. The Federation of Bosnia and Hercegovina

My fifth and sixth assignments in Bosnia took place in the Federation of Bosnia and Hercegovina, the other of the two entities, on the south side of the inter-entity boundary line (or IEBL) from the Serbian Republic where I had been for the third and fourth assignments.

In June 1998 I was recruited to be an international trainer in Jablanica, a couple of hours south of the capital city of Sarajevo. Jablanica is a small town in a beautiful setting, nestled in the hills and mountains. The sparkling blue and icy cold waters of the Neretva River flow through the town and there is a freshwater lake nestled above the town. I was delighted with the topography, which reminded me a bit of Banff, Alberta, an hour drive from my hometown of Calgary.

Working for the OSCE on a long-term assignment of six months, as this was, I had the use of their fleet of white Pajero jeeps. So when I had time off, I drove up to the lake to swim. I love being in water and swimming for exercise. What a bonus it was to be able to do this during my time in Jablanica! However, respect for the environment was not a characteristic I observed in Bosnia. In a post-conflict state, ecology is not the top priority. Although the lake water was pleasant in many ways, what I did not enjoy were the floating plastic bottles of all sizes! I tried to swim around them but it was close to impossible. I only hoped that any bacteria they might be carrying would be well enough diluted by the volume of water in the lake. There must have been some truth to that theory as I never did develop a malady.

Again, I rented an apartment on my own. It was conveniently located close to our OSCE office so I could walk to work instead of driving. Given that Jablanica was a small town, our office was not very big and I remember all of the staff. The internationals were probably the only foreigners in town! My colleagues were young: a British fellow was our human rights officer; and a Greek–American woman covered democratization. The elections officer was from Eastern Europe, perhaps Bulgaria again, but an easier character than his countryman with whom I'd had dealings on the fourth assignment. The core supervisor was a Canadian man. At 48, I was the elder in the office!

As the international trainer, I had the good fortune to work with a genuinely lovely Bosnian woman of my age, Sadeta Begtasevic who was the local trainer. She too had been a teacher of French – what a coincidence! Sadeta and her husband Zoran were not from the same ethnic group. Before the conflict, their bi-ethnic marriage was not noteworthy, but post-conflict it was another matter. Nevertheless, they were a strong and happy couple, who set an excellent example of inter-ethnic harmony.

Sadeta and Zoran lived in Konjic, where he had been the mayor. It was a half hour's drive north of Jablanica, and they had a *vikendica* (a small summer chalet) at another lake up in the mountains. I was lucky enough to visit them at both their home in the town and at the lake. The water was colder but much cleaner, and that made the swimming more pleasant.

Some 16 years later in 2016 in Ottawa I was able to get news of Sadeta. Through friends, I met Svjetlana, who had grown up in Konjic and was now a Canadian citizen. When we were chatting, we were both amazed to find out I knew her hometown. Subsequently, she was going back to visit family in Bosnia and she contacted Sadeta in Konjic. I love these small-world discoveries. Even better, Sadeta and

I actually got to speak to each other just as I was doing the final editing of my story. I felt really happy to reconnect with her after some 20 years.

Two other local staff I remember were Mersiha and Leyla, and I got news of them from Sadeta when we spoke. Mersiha had worked with the Red Cross during and after the conflict to help people find their relatives when they had been involuntarily separated. I know this because she tried to help me find Martino, the Yugoslav man I mentioned in the chapter on Ethiopia. Oddly enough I was finally able to locate him myself. I was writing Christmas cards – yes, in 1998, I still did that by hand – and I was using an old-fashioned address book. Lo and behold, I found Martino's name there! Better still, I visited him in Sarajevo on Christmas Day – a happy reunion some ten years after we had first met! I was staying in the capital city with good friends to this day, Dawn Wood-Memic and Almir Memic, who had welcomed me for the holidays.

Another good memory from my time in Jablanica was getting to know one of the election supervisors, Bela Kapur from London, England. As a lawyer, among other things, Bela was well suited to the work the OSCE was doing and she ended up being hired to work for them in Sarajevo. I was delighted to have a new pal and we had some fun adventures together. We went on holiday with a friend of hers to Sicily, a most refreshing change of scene. Years later we are still friends, meeting up with others in 2018 in the Netherlands for a bike and barge tour. What a lovely bonus from the Jablanica assignment!

The six-month assignment in Jablanica morphed into a subsequent assignment as an elections officer in the same southerly region of the country but in another small town, Capljina. I had a very cute apartment on the top floor of a small hotel where I hosted my annual Boxing Day birthday party. Pals came from as far away as Sarajevo, over a couple of hours drive away. They included Canadian friends Jeanette Stovel, Nelson Nip and their two young children of whom I was very fond.

The majority population in Capljina was Croat, i.e., Catholic; in Jablanica it was Bosniak. In an effort to accommodate both ethnicities of my guests, for my festive spread I had tried to buy salami that did not contain pork. However, once in the shop I realized I did not have the Serbo-Croatian vocabulary I needed. So I tried the German word for pig but was not sure I had been understood. Instead, I have this hilarious memory of trying to imitate a pig by making a snorting noise and then holding my index fingers in an X to show I did not want any pork in the salami. To this day I do not know if I was successful. In writing this tale, I wonder now if the shopkeeper knew what I was trying to communicate but was actually revelling in the ridiculous effort I was making!

One of the fascinating aspects of election administration in Bosnia was the need to visit remote communities to assess their capacity and readiness to stage a safe and fair electoral process. The Capljina office was responsible for the small village of Ravno to the southeast. In kilometres it was not far away but I remember the trip took at least an hour because it was on a single-track road along the side of a steep hill. It was not a straight road so you had to approach the blind curves slowly to avoid running into an oncoming vehicle. Perhaps because of this challenging access to the town, the residents were not used to visitors and were not very welcoming. Fortunately though, we were able to conduct our business, and return to the office with the information we then passed on to the local electoral authorities, thus sparing them the time-consuming and risky journey.

The Capljina gig lasted only a couple of months, as I was then asked to take on the role of senior election officer at the OSCE Regional Centre in Mostar. I accepted with delight. I was more than ready for the full responsibility of the international elections staff in the five affiliated field offices. This new role began in early 1999.

In June 1999 I took a five-day Foundation Course in the Theory and Conduct of Democratic Elections offered by the University of Essex and delivered in Sarajevo. It was an intense week of learning the theory behind what my colleagues and I were already implementing. It was an excellent technical diversion from the day-to-day reality of election administration in a post-conflict environment.

Because election dates kept slipping, I ended up staying in Mostar for two years. The initial six-month assignment that began in Jablanica in June 1998 turned into two and a half years in that region. It was well worth every minute, even though it was interrupted in the last year by a herniated disc in my lower back. That resulted in my being medevacked to Ottawa in April 2000. What a journey that was, but how fortunate I was to get a diagnosis so quickly. That would never have happened had I been in Canada.

The pain began on a Thursday. It was completely unexpected, although it did happen shortly after the intense country-wide elections were finally held. If it was stress related, that was certainly part of the cause. It was also entirely unfamiliar, as I was an active, healthy individual.

I could not find relief in any position, not sitting, standing or lying down. By Monday morning I was desperate, having had no rest for four days and nights. My local colleagues took me to see a doctor who ordered an X-ray. The prescription was to rest for two weeks. I burst into tears. Resting was not something I knew how to do. As luck would have it, Monday was the day the Swiss doctor, recruited by the OSCE, visited our regional centre. He decided I needed to return to Sarajevo with him for further tests. The two-hour ride there in his jeep was extremely uncomfortable. That same evening, I had a CAT scan which resulted in a prognosis from a German military surgeon – either I was to have a back operation in Bosnia or I was to go home. Although not a pleasant choice, it was nonetheless an easy one. I went home.

Two days later I was on a private jet, accompanied by a doctor from Egypt. He traveled the full distance with me. At Heathrow Airport in London, I was taken to the equivalent of a four-bed hospital room to await my British Airways flight to Montreal. I flew first class so that I could be horizontal, which was better for my back apparently. It also meant champagne was available and the good doctor agreed I could have some. It was a pretty smooth ride. From Montreal I was transported in an ambulance for the remaining two hours to get to the Civic Hospital in Ottawa.

When these arrangements were being made in Sarajevo, I told the German military officer working on my case about Canada's socialized medical care. I was concerned that I would not get to see a surgeon there. His response was, "Karen, I think if you arrive by ambulance, having been medevacked from Europe, someone will see you." And of course, he was right.

A Canadian neurosurgeon informed me that a back operation would have an 80 to 90 per cent success rate but he thought I could recover without surgery. I didn't want to be part of the other 10 to 20 per cent so I began three months of physiotherapy, successfully avoiding back surgery. I was delighted to return to my job and home in Mostar for the last six months of 2000.

In Mostar I was fortunate enough to live in a self-contained one-bedroom apartment on the ground floor of an older couple's home. It was sweet. I had my own patio outside my private entrance with a fig tree that bore one of my favourite fruits. There is nothing quite like a fig right off the tree. It is completely unrelated to the filling in Fig Newtons, a healthy cookie, which no doubt dates me and any readers who know this old stand-by from a former era.

My Mostar home was particularly comfortable in the heat of summer, being on the ground floor, but chilly in the winter without adequate heating. Electric stand-up heaters just do not cut the cold, even though the temperature seldom fell below freezing.

The town of Mostar is an historic one. It is home to a UNESCO World Heritage Site, the beautiful stone bridge over the Neretva River, which flows down from the mountains south of Sarajevo through the towns of Konjic and Jablanica. The Mostar Bridge was 427 years old when it was destroyed in 1993 during the conflict, and physically separated the east and west sides of the Bosniak (i.e., Muslim) community in Mostar. Further to the west but still in Mostar lived the Croat majority. Mostar was torn apart during the conflict and signs of the destruction were evident along the western shores of the Neretva. The OSCE Regional Centre was located in this area, which was claimed by the Croats after the conflict. A Bosniak cemetery was just down the street from the office. I walked past it daily on my way to and from work.

The Mostar Bridge, known locally as *Stari Most* (literally Old Bridge), was eventually restored by UNESCO and reopened in 2004. During my time in Mostar (1999-2000), a temporary suspension bridge contributed to the gradual reconciliation between the two sides. An annual tradition of diving off the Mostar

111

Bridge began in 1968. It is 24 meters down into water that is icy even at the end of July. Its temperature has been recorded as low as seven degrees Celsius!

One year I observed the event which involved both diving and what is known as the cannonball. In Bosnia they are performed in the opposite way from North America. Normally, at least in my experience, a dive is rated on how little water is splashed upon the diver's entry to the water, whereas the opposite is true for a cannonball. This was reversed when I watched it. The dive was a swan dive, creating a big splash and looked like a very painful way to enter the water from that height. The cannonball was rated according to how little splash there was. From what I have learned from kayakers on the Pacific Ocean, which is eight degrees Celsius off Victoria, British Columbia, cold water shock can be deadly. In fact, there have been deaths among the divers plummeting into the Neretva. Nowadays, jumping off the bridge is a tourist attraction!

The head of our Mostar office was a retired American ambassador who ran his ship much as he would have his former embassies. The senior officers of each department met with him as a team every morning for a briefing, which was actually a great communication tactic. Security was often at the top of the agenda but by early 1999 things were relatively calm. Still, Mostar was a politically divided city with six distinct municipalities, three of which were Bosniak and three Croat. To say the least, this made political life in the city interesting not to mention challenging, which is why it took so many months to prepare for municipal elections. Once they finally took place in April 2000, the results had to be implemented – not an easy task and definitely an all-consuming one.

112

Again, because of the relative longevity of this final assignment in Bosnia, I was able to make some solid friendships. The most lasting ones were those made with fellow expatriates from many countries: Italy, Switzerland, France, Estonia and the US, to name a few. We were from many professions as well. In Canada, I rarely associate with police officers, for example, but in such an insecure environment, they were there in spades. As their pals there, we learned a lot about what that profession requires from its representatives. Although there are bad apples in every line of work, I had the pleasure of meeting some of the *crème de la crème* and I am the richer for it. With some we are still in contact, even if only via social media. We passed many hours together, both at work and at play.

Mostar in the late 1990s had some up-market shops such as Benetton, whose logo was 'United Colors of Benetton'. During my recovery from the herniated disc, I managed to lose about 25 pounds, reducing the load on my arthritic back. A new body image is a great motivator for retail therapy and so I indulged. My main physical attribute is probably my long legs, which of course can be best shown off by a mini skirt! Yes, I succumbed, with not one but two of them. They were made of pleather, i.e., fake leather. One was black, and in true Benetton fashion, the other was purple, one of my favourite colours.

I was in Bosnia for four consecutive Halloweens, which I happen to love because everyone has an excuse to be goofy. An American expat had opened a pub in Mostar and one Halloween I tried to dress up as Tina Turner, minus the wig unfortunately. But the legs were definitely on display under the skimpy mini skirt. One of the other revelers, male of course, on sizing me up said, "That's a nice belt you're wearing!" Another man in my life, my father in fact, had stated at my fiftieth birthday party in Calgary, "That skirt is absolutely obscene!" I thanked him for the compliment!

Mostar had an outdoor swimming pool that had managed to survive the conflict intact. Returning to Bosnia in July after my recuperation in Ottawa, I delighted in the opportunity to continue my fitness routine by swimming lengths at the pool after work. I remember local women were often hanging out in the bleachers. They watched me swim and when I had finished, I always got a nod of approval. I felt on top of the world. That can happen after a physical challenge has laid you low and you eventually manage to come back to the surface. The resulting contrast in your state of health is exhilarating.

Another pastime among us expats was the hour-long drive from Mostar to the Dalmatian coast of Croatia along the Adriatic Sea of the Mediterranean. I don't know how many times I made that journey. I loved the towns along the coast and the nearby islands too. All the way to the south, just north of Croatia's border with Montenegro, lay the Balkan jewel of Dubrovnik, a walled city along the sea and a UNESCO World Heritage Site.

In the late 1990s, Dubrovnik was still recovering from the conflict so was not overrun by tourists. To my eyes, coming from war-torn Mostar, the external damage to Dubrovnik's infrastructure appeared minimal. After all, the small city is fortified by solid stone walls, half of which back onto the sea. I thought it had stood up to the conflict quite well. The low number of tourists was probably more related to security concerns, i.e., that it might not be safe in terms of ongoing tensions but this was not at all evident, nor did I ever feel unsafe there.

I took countless trips to Dubrovnik. The first time was with one of my Swiss military colleagues. It was December, when the temperatures can be chilly so swimming was not in the plans; however, my companion decided that he wanted to test the waters, and so he did! Fortunately for me, I had a head cold and was able to use that as an excuse not to join him.

I managed to find a comfortable place to stay when visiting Dubrovnik. It was conveniently located just outside the north entrance of the walled town and was only about $20 a night for a bed and a shared bathroom. I forget if this included breakfast but probably not or I would have remembered. The elderly landlady lived there alone, I believe, in the large house so it was a sensible way to bring in some income. She didn't speak English so I really had to work hard on my weak Croatian, especially when I had to phone her to reserve a bed or two.

I do like to skinny dip. I have two memories of being able to do this in the summer heat of Dubrovnik. Both times it was in the darkness of night. One dip took place near my accommodation with my good friend Bela. Like many of my friends in that era, she was about 20 years younger. She was quite taken aback by my child-like penchant for fun – this adventure included! It was delightful slipping into the cooling waters of the Adriatic under night's black cover. The other dip was with my Greek–French elections colleague and a few others, over near the port of the town, but again well after midnight. Ah, it was so refreshing!

Another such incident occurred up the shore from Dubrovnik but first I need to set the stage. I had just returned to Dubrovnik by ferry from a visit to Bari, Italy where the family of my good friend, Gabriella (Gabry) Danza, lived. They had hosted me and took me to yet another UNESCO World Heritage Site in nearby

Puglia: the Trulli are prehistoric buildings characterized by circular white stone walls, small windows and spectacular pinnacles. About 1,500 Trulli still function as houses, hotels and shops. Gabry's family sent me back to Bosnia with a wheeled cart loaded down with Italian food delicacies for her. An American police officer friend in Mostar had agreed to drive down to Dubrovnik to pick me up. Rob came with his colleague, Gail. A new adventure was about to begin.

I can't remember the month, just that it was hot. We needed a swim and I knew just where to go as we traveled back to Mostar from Dubrovnik. Sandy beaches are the exception in Croatia where the shoreline is mostly rocky but near the town of Ston there is a lovely sandy beach called Prapratno. For some reason, few people were around that day. Perhaps it was later in the afternoon. It was not dark but I knew that nudity was allowed on this beach and so I indulged. Rob was much too modest to join me but at some point the wind must have changed and the next thing we knew Rob was immersed in the water, proudly holding up his swimming trunks! In fact, he was swinging them around his head in the excitement of the moment. Cool. He was enjoying himself.

Next however, I heard Gail calling, "Houston, we have a problem!" And indeed we did. Rob's car keys had been in the pocket of his trunks but of course they were no longer there. He was chest deep in the water and the keys were buried somewhere in the soft sand within the radius of the swirling trunks. We couldn't find them. What to do? Well, first of all, we donned our swimsuits. Next, I had to put my limited local language skills to use. I knew the word for key and some young locals with snorkeling masks took on the job.

What would we do if they couldn't find the precious keys? Not only would we be stranded without transportation part way home to Mostar, still a fair distance away, but all the food in the carefully packed cart would spoil in the heat of the locked car. Fortunately, luck was with us, and one of the young fellows found the keys. What a relief! This was not one of the risks normally associated with skinny dipping!

However, I can be a creative gal, and I did have another such experience. It took place on the delightful island of Mljet, which is a car ferry ride away from Dubrovnik. I only visited once but the memory is both strong and positive. Three of us took a long weekend to explore Mljet. Our first adventure was the most unusual.

On arriving on the island, we were driving around to check it out and came upon a parking lot near the large inland sea. We parked under some trees, far from the shore and walked over to check out the swimming options. Bela was already in her bathing suit and wasted no time getting in the water. It was midday and very hot. I was tempted to go in but didn't want to get my shorts and T-shirt wet, nor was I willing to walk all the way back to the car to get my bathing suit. Bela was well out into the lake by this time. So, you guessed it, I removed almost all my clothing but decided to stick with a modicum of decency by leaving on my underpants. I was in, and swimming out to join Bela.

I may not have mentioned that I also like to swim long distances. Before we knew it, Bela and I were already almost halfway across the lake. On the other side was a picturesque monastery. What was the point in swimming back to shore when it looked almost as far to swim to the other side? Mutual decision made, we beckoned to Heidi, who was becoming just a small dot on the shore. She was hesitating but eventually

117

joined us in her bra and panties. What a contingent we were! We made it to the other side but not without a few tense moments when the water got a bit rough and Heidi started to panic. I managed to coax her across because by then we were closer to the other side.

But now what? We were very grateful to have made it safely across but we were dehydrated and had no money to buy a drink from the concession stands outside the monastery. Fortunately for us, Bela's foreign language skills were good, and of course, she was the only one wearing a proper bathing suit. She succeeded in bringing back Cokes for all of us – what charm she had obviously turned on! Furthermore, she had learned there was a small boat to take us back to the shore where we had carelessly left our clothes and car keys. Hoping our possessions were still waiting for us, she would then be able to reimburse the boatman. Heidi was happy to take the boat as was Bela, given that both of them had their bodies more adequately covered than I did. But I could not bring myself to get on board in my utilitarian underpants. I swam back!

Another very strong memory of my time in Bosnia and in a different season was spending Christmas Eve in Sarajevo in the company of our Swiss mission colleagues. That evening at their camp we enjoyed a delicious cheese fondue. I could feel the sadness among some of the Swiss because they were far away from their families. I don't recall how we passed the time between dinner and midnight but the mass itself at that hour was memorable. It was a cold and snowy night. After the service as we filed out of the cathedral, they were giving out small glasses of Bosnian slivovitz, the potent plum brandy. How well it went down on that frosty dark night, loaded with the emotions of the Christmas season!

My final assignment in Bosnia ended in December 2000 and resulted in one of the most difficult goodbyes ever. I remember being picked up from my cozy Mostar home by the OSCE driver who would take me to the airport. As we pulled away from the place I had called home for almost two years, I remember thinking, "I don't want to do this anymore. It is just too hard to have to leave behind the life I have created in this home away from home." Did I succeed in listening to myself? You can probably guess that I didn't. If I have not said it before, I will say it now, "What doesn't kill you makes you stronger!"

Episode I, Chapter 1: My 1st 20 years

Mum and me, 1953

Mum at Barbara Christie Needle Arts in Calgary

Karen Christie

Mum, Dad and me en route from Toronto to Calgary, April 1950

High school graduation, 1967

Dad and me, 1953

Episode II, Chapters 2-6: My 20s

Picking strawberries in Norway

With the Haug family on the school boat

With my students in Dawson City, mid 1970s

Summiting Ayers Rock, Australia

Karen Christie

Yukon River canoe trip, 1976

Cycling in Norway, 1981

On the Heaphy Track, NZ, 1971

Cycling in Korea, 1979

Cycling in Bali, 1979

Episode III, Chapters 7-9: My 30s

With my ESL class, Queen Elizabeth Jr/Sr High School, Calgary

Hiking with ESL students on Tunnel Mountain, Banff, Alberta

Field trip to Expo 86, Vancouver, Canada

Karen Christie

Arba Minch Water Technology Institute (AWTI), Ethiopia, 1987-88

AWTI colleagues, Ethiopia

In the AWTI classroom

Promoting women in Ethiopia

Ready to drive from Calgary to Ottawa, 1989

Episode IV, Chapters 10-14: My 40s

WUSC office in Ottawa, mid 1990s

With colleagues and host family, Maglaj

Voter registration in Maglaj, Bosnia and Herzegovina, 1997

Destroyed building, Maglaj, Bosnia and Herzegovina

Karen Christie

Neretva River, Mostar, Bosnia and Herzegovina

With Sadeta and Zoran overlooking Mostar

'Benetton babe' with friend Rob

Reunited with Martino, from Ethiopia to Bosnia

Six Continents Over Five Decades

Field trip in OSCE vehicle, Kosovo

Receiving UN Peacekeeping Medal from MP

Forest fire, on vacation in Montenegro

Kandahar Provincial Reconstruction Team (KPRT), Afghanistan

Karen Christie

Adrenalin junkie in a Cougar helicopter

With Cdn. Forces colleague, KPRT

Women's *shura* at KPRT

KPRT 'reservoir' at January 1st fundraiser

Episode VI, Chapters 21-22: My 60s

My 'blast-pod' in Kabul, Afghanistan, at the door...inside

Socializing on blast-pod deck

With Afghan Minister of Education, 2011   With RCMP on Remembrance Day

With colleagues and Gov. General David Johnston, Christmas Eve, 2011

Our education team visit to Herat, Afghanistan, 2012

School girls in Herat

Snacks on spa day at my residence in Port-au-Prince, Haiti

Karen Christie

My 3rd medal, Canadian Embassy in Haiti

With Dad, showing off our 5 medals

Enjoying Cote des Arcadins, Haiti

Club Indigo, Cote des Arcadins

Pam and me at Cyvadier Plage near Jacmel, Haiti

Spa day, residence in Port-au-Prince

Where I broke my arm

Haitian police plaque, Embassy office

Happy camper after almost 3 years in Haiti

Karen Christie

Epilogue: 'Refired!'

'Refirement', where the livin' is easy! Cowichan River, Canada

EPISODE V

My 50s in Europe and Asia

15. More in the Former Yugoslavia

After the emotional farewell to Bosnia in December 2000, I seriously wanted to avoid creating another such situation. So when 2001 dawned in Ottawa, I was determined to settle in Canada after my extended absence of almost four years in Bosnia. Job searching is never easy and, in that era, international experience overseas was not a highly valued commodity in Ottawa. Add to that, at 50 years of age, I was no longer a spring chicken!

Fortunately, I managed to get an interesting contract with my former employer, the Association of Canadian Community Colleges, which now exists under the name of Colleges and Institutes Canada. The contract was temporary so I continued to network in the interests of finding something to provide a stronger anchor. Apparently, it was not meant to be.

My work in Bosnia had taught me to be more politically astute. One reality that became an issue was that my time in Bosnia had never been particularly well compensated financially. I had no salary per se but I did receive a per diem in US dollars seven days a week. As such, it was not taxable, and it resulted in my receiving about the same as a net salary in Canada. In reality, it was sufficient, especially given the relatively low cost of living in war-torn Bosnia.

Nevertheless, it was particularly jarring to work with much younger colleagues who were receiving a salary as well as a per diem. For example, in 1998, a British colleague, who was a peer in terms of our level of responsibility, was earning 44,000 pounds sterling plus the per diem for his work. This just did not seem fair so I was motivated to write to my Member of Parliament, Liberal Mauril Bélanger, asking that this inequity be addressed. Unfortunately, in my time in Bosnia it was not. However, through the link I had made to my MP's office, I eventually managed to get a short-term assignment as an election observer, not supervisor, in Montenegro in April 2001 with my former employer, the OSCE. This was an excellent experience and a satisfactory consequence of my lobbying efforts.

In June 2001, my friend Marianne, who had first sent me to Bosnia in 1996, offered me a job continuing my work in election administration but this time in Kosovo and still with the Organization for Security and Cooperation in Europe (OSCE). At first, I was vehement in telling her I was not interested since I wanted to remain in Canada, but the carrot she held out was pretty enticing. The offer to go back to the former Yugoslavia came complete with a salary and a per diem! It was impossible to resist. I succumbed and off I went for another six-month assignment, under the CIDA-funded Balkan Civilian Deployment Project. It was worth it, in many ways.

I will mention here an important factor that facilitated my absences from Canada. At the end of 1995, I bought a new townhouse in Ottawa so I had a base until I left that city permanently in 2016 to move to Canada's west coast. During my forays overseas, I rented my furnished Ottawa home to friends. I was able to create a win-win scenario for both renter and landlady (*moi*)! I made the master bedroom available for the renter and set myself up in the smaller guest bedroom. In return for the low rent, the deal was that I could continue to use that street address and stay there on a temporary basis when I was in Ottawa on vacation. This suited both of us very well.

But back to my saga. Although overseas experience may have been less valued in Canada at the time, it was not the case when I was recruited for another overseas assignment. On arrival in June 2001 in Pristina, the capital of Kosovo, I was immediately named the senior elections officer in the politically divided town of Mitrovica, about an hour drive to the north. After all, in Bosnia, I had lived in another politically divided town, Mostar, so it was an obvious fit. In Mitrovica in Kosovo, the Ibar River formed the boundary of an ethnic divide. To the south was the Kosovar Albanian majority and to the north were the minority Kosovar Bosnians and Serbs.

The OSCE Regional Centre was on the south side of the river but I initially took accommodation on the other side. By then, I was able to communicate in Serbo-Croatian but I knew no Albanian. This arrangement did not last for long as I soon learned it was not always possible to cross the bridge to get home, due to security concerns. So I moved to an apartment practically next door to the office, which made it pretty close to perfect.

However, I heard an alarming story about an international peacekeeper from another Slavic country working in Kosovo. Apparently, he had spoken Serbian in the wrong place at the wrong time and had been shot by the Kosovar Albanians. In other words, it was not necessarily a good idea to express myself in Serbian outside Serb enclaves. Well, it was easier said than done after four years in Bosnia speaking Serbo-Croatian.

I will always remember the morning when my landlord, who was Albanian, came to see me at my apartment. When I opened the door, I greeted him with, "Good morning." but it was in Serbian. As soon as I realized my error, I clamped my hand over my mouth. Of course, I was not in danger in that setting but it was a good reminder to be more careful about when Serbian popped out of my mouth. In fact, I did eventually learn that in some circumstances, and in a respectful way, I could use Serbian, especially with older Albanians because it was their second language.

That linguistic skill was especially useful one summer day when I had been over on the north side of the Ibar River in a large Serb enclave. I had driven myself to a nearby lake in the region to have a swim. I encountered some colleagues there and we had a lovely afternoon. They left ahead of me, as I wanted to go for a walk along a road just a bit above the lake. I was really enjoying myself, singing happily, when out of nowhere, a large German shepherd appeared and bit me behind the knee! I was astonished as I had not even seen him. Perhaps he had been lying peacefully by the side of the road and my noisy approach had startled him.

The dog's bite had drawn blood and I remembered being concerned that my white ankle socks would be soiled! Honestly, what comes to mind at a time like that! I wiped away the blood with my hands as I was worried that using lake water might not be sanitary. I then looked about to see what I should do next as I was still a distance from my vehicle. I saw there were two people down by the lake. I called out to them but I didn't know how to say in Serbian that the dog had bitten me. So instead, I said, "That dog is bad." They approached and could see what had happened so they led me to a *veekendica* (a small chalet) where there was an older couple. A local remedy was in order. I was treated with homemade *rakija*, the powerful plum brandy, which wiped my wound clean and was also applied internally, helping me to recover from the shock!

After some rest, my rescuers accompanied me to my vehicle so I could return to Mitrovica, a 45-minute drive away. I radioed the regional centre, which in turn contacted the French security forces responsible for the stability in the region. I was to report to their headquarters for further treatment in case the dog had rabies.

I have to acknowledge here that I had not attended to getting my shots before this mission. This was partly because of Kosovo being part of Europe, and it just never occurred to me that there would be any need for a rabies shot for a European trip. This meant the French military had to use their limited provisions on a civilian who was not even one of their nationals! I received five shots that afternoon, one in each limb, and I am not sure where the last one was administered. I was required to lie there on one of their cots for a couple of hours as I recall. I had not indicated that I spoke French, although I don't know why as I am not usually shy about that sort of thing. Anyway, the soldiers continued speaking French within my hearing and I heard them complaining that I was using up their precious medical resources.

I needed follow-up shots for a couple of months after that. Obviously, I did not contract rabies from the dog bite, thank goodness. It had been an odd incident though. While still in Canada before my departure for Kosovo, I had had a nasty dream that I might possibly die there. That did not bode particularly well as you can imagine. I went anyway but lying in that military clinic I was saying to myself, "I can't believe this is how I'm going to die! My family will be so upset." Fortunately, it was not necessary to send that message to them.

Working in Kosovo after four years in Bosnia was fascinating. In some ways, it was a microcosm of the other conflict but it was no less complicated. The major conflict was between Albanians and Serbs with some Bosnians in the mix and ethnic tensions were high. The OSCE was there to help the Kosovars hold parliamentary elections on November 17, 2001. As in Bosnia, I was responsible for managing international elections personnel in half a dozen field offices on both sides of the Ibar River. I also had the role of liaising with internationals from other organizations such as the military and the police to make sure we each stayed in our lanes, to use a military expression, on election day.

Living conditions were difficult because the power went out often and this in turn affected the water supply, which was not even drinkable because of lead contamination. In addition, temperatures became uncomfortable as winter moved in and the buildings had no central heating. On top of this were the constant security concerns which affected our freedom of movement to do our jobs.

To deal with these inconvenient realities, we found ways to escape to other places. On one occasion two of my OSCE colleagues and I went to Sveti Stefan, further south along the Adriatic in Montenegro where I had been briefly as an elections observer early in the year. It was a long drive but a very picturesque one, and a welcome diversion. But we did not know this was not going to be a particularly restful break. Why, you might ask? What could possibly go wrong? Well, a forest fire that was burning out of control to the north had a considerable impact. We watched it in the daytime and as the winds picked up, we became increasingly nervous. It did result in some unusual sunsets though, with the air so heavy with smoke.

It was perhaps our second night there when the owner of the pension came banging on our door sometime before midnight. He told us it might not be safe for us to stay there, with the fires approaching. Of course, we were alarmed. Where were we to go? To make matters worse, one of us had taken the car to visit some new acquaintances. He was far enough away that our hand-held Motorola radios did not reach him and our cell phone providers didn't offer service in Montenegro.

I will admit that Marie and I panicked. We quickly gathered some of our possessions and left the building. On the street, the scent of smoke was strong and very concerning. My first thought was to hitchhike but I did not get good vibes from the sole male driver that stopped, so I declined his offer. Who knew where he might take us under the cover of night? In these extreme circumstances, we didn't want to add insult to injury.

So now what? Finally, we decided to go down to the stony beach and try to seek shelter from the advancing fire there. It was a dreadful situation. I had visions of having to go into the water to get away from the flames, if they came that close. At least we would probably survive but our passports would not. And then we would be soaking wet and cold. Thankfully, it never came to that but we spent a very long and restless night on the beach. We finally reconnected with our other friend in the morning and decided that it was time to drive back to the relative comfort of Kosovo! Honestly, I never want to be in such a situation again.

We were all affected by America's 9/11 in September that year. Kosovo is six hours ahead of New York. I had just returned to the office that afternoon around 3:00 p.m. and out in the parking area, someone told me the twin towers had been attacked. Out of context, I was not sure what they were talking about, especially since I was in a place where buildings were often attacked. Across the river in the Bosnian majority area was a complex of three apartment buildings, so I was confused as to why they were being called the 'twin towers'. The news gradually sank in.

Later that afternoon, I was scheduled to drive down to Pristina for a social event with a friend. I was allowed to travel but on arrival there, my friend, who was American, was not interested in socializing. Instead, we watched TV for whatever coverage we could get on what had happened in New York. We were anxious in particular about possible repercussions on a Muslim-majority population such as the one in Kosovo. Nothing concrete happened at that time but many of my colleagues, Americans and other nationalities, were sombre and worried both personally and on a global level. I was actually surprised when an American police officer, who had become a friend, expressed an opinion I did not expect to hear. It was along the lines of what does America expect when they are at liberty to drop bombs on other countries? We were all aware of how the world was changing and that America was not immune to the ever-present challenges.

On a more upbeat note, another memory is well worth recounting. As I have mentioned, with colleagues of many nationalities and many skill levels, not to mention languages, working together in a conflict-ridden environment towards a set-in-stone major event is a recipe that leads to a high level of stress. That said, we got to know each other pretty well, and the elections took place in mid-November in a relatively calm environment.

During the intense preparations we had talked about how we would celebrate once our task was done. One person on my team was a retired British major who had a good sense of humour. He thought it would be a great opportunity for his team of core supervisors to get together afterwards and do a full Monty, a take-off on a British film with a great music track. For those who might not know, a full Monty refers to a line-up of men doing a striptease act in front of an audience. The only article of clothing is a hat which is put to use to cover up the bare essentials! I wasn't enamoured with this idea but I figured it was unlikely to happen.

The scene was set: a locally owned restaurant a few doors away from the office. We booked it for the evening and gathered there for food, drink and celebration. Someone brought the CD of the full Monty, and before we knew it, it was playing. Fortunately, the windows to the street were covered up with paper, given that drinking is not compatible with Islam and the owner would not like to be exposed, so to speak. Well, unfortunately for him, and perhaps also for us, here is what happened.

Three of the core supervisors were ready to carry out the deed: the retired British major, a young Spaniard, and a retired Canadian RCMP in his official red serge uniform (don't ask me why!). They were up on a table in the restaurant, the music of Full Monty playing loud and clear. Sure enough, the dear Brit went all the way, to the horror of many of us gathered there, me in particular, since I was his boss!

I had been standing with my back to the windows, a young Albanian man beside me. He had a baseball cap on and I desperately asked him if he would provide his hat to cover the essentials of the about-to-be-naked man in front of us. He was horrified at the thought although the other option was just as unappealing. In the end, he surrendered his hat for the decency, or some variation of it, of the very inebriated and very naked man who had forgotten that part of the movie where you are supposed to have a hat for the 'procedure'.

As an aside, the retired RCMP came to apologize, as I recall, that he had not done the full Monty because he could not get his knee-high boots off! I was not at all upset about that, but instead very grateful. Needless to say, the Brit was not in good shape the next day, behaving in a rather sheepish manner, understandably. Fortunately, there were no other consequences, at least not to my knowledge.

We worked for another month or so after the elections to ensure the implementation of the election results. In that time, I managed to fit in a brief R&R (rest & recreation) in Istanbul. I had not been there before and I found it intriguing. It was a special time because it was Ramadan and so we were present when the Turks broke their fast at sunset each night. One day we were in the big city market at sunset and all thoughts of sales were put aside in order to eat the first meal since breakfast, which had been consumed before sunrise. It was early December and the hours of daylight were short, creating a mystical feel as twilight drew to a close, shrouding the lights of the beautiful Blue Mosque, an Istanbul landmark.

The sun was also setting on the assignment but with a new adventure on the horizon. My faithful friend Marianne had yet another job for me, again with salary and per diem, in the neighbouring Former Yugoslav Republic of Macedonia. This made goodbyes from Kosovo much easier as I would still be in the 'hood.

It is appropriate here to mention that the same former colleague, Marianne, who had become a friend, was responsible for my receiving a Peacekeeping Medal for my time in Kosovo. She had pursued the national Canadian authorities and jumped through bureaucratic hoops to make it possible for the Canadian military to award medals to civilians for their work on peacekeeping missions.

As you can imagine, this took some time but it yielded positive results. Four years after I left Kosovo, I received the UN Peacekeeping Medal in 2005 in the office of my MP in Ottawa, Mauril Bélanger, who sadly is no longer with us. Although it was a small, intimate ceremony, it was a proud and emotional moment for me. One of my best friends in Ottawa, Lieutenant Colonel (now retired) Doug Cargo, was there by my side as I received the honour. In Calgary, my father, who had received two medals for his service in the Second World War, was pretty pumped about his daughter getting a medal for her work as a civilian. Little did we know there would be more of these to come.

16. Expertise in Election Administration

By the end of 2001, I had held five different positions in election administration in the same number of years in the former Yugoslavia. They had all been under the auspices of the Organization for Security and Cooperation in Europe (OSCE). As I mentioned, my increasing international experience in elections in post-conflict environments gave me serious 'street cred' in the overseas arena, even if it was less likely to be recognized in Canada. (I did finally find a home for that expertise in the Canadian government but that is a later chapter.)

Now it was time to contribute to another organization, this time an American one, but still in the Balkans. This was the International Foundation for Electoral Systems, or IFES, as it is known. I was to become the deputy director of its country office in Skopje, the capital city of the Former Yugoslav Republic of Macedonia. It was quite a smooth transition from Kosovo where I was working until late 2001. My new one-year assignment began in January 2002. I was fortunate to still be contracted through the Balkan Civilian Deployment Project, funded by the Canadian government, so I again had a salary and a per diem, making it a sweet deal financially.

But this assignment was sweet in many ways. It was the first time I was to live in the capital city of the country where I was working. This meant that there were lots more perks such as arts and culture, restaurants, and even something as simple as a much larger population. I had the nicest (and most expensive) accommodation of the past five years – half the upper floor of a large house built by an architect.

His parents lived on the ground floor and he and his wife, a dentist, lived on the second floor with their two teenage children. There were two apartments on the top floor with lovely views of the mountain that towers over Skopje. It is called Vodno, and I often went walking up there.

My apartment was modern and fun. There were three smallish bedrooms, one of which was in a loft accessed by a drop-down ladder! I felt a little more grown up living here, perhaps an odd observation but let's just say I was no longer roughing it. My mother even came from Calgary for a visit. And I enjoyed my neighbours: the owners of course, and the Canadian woman, Michelle Berg, who lived in the apartment next to mine. Life was good, and comfortable! A bonus was that I could walk to work from home, instead of depending on drivers to come and pick me up.

The IFES office was the usual hive of electoral activity. Although it was not our responsibility to run the parliamentary elections to be held in 2002, we played the role of mentor to, and watch dog of, the national electoral authorities. IFES also assumed an active role in coordinating the external electoral assistance of some 12-plus international donors. Our funder was the US Agency for International Development (USAID), whose financial contribution to IFES was in the form of a grant. I found that to be noticeably different from the way the Canadian government usually offers financing.

Up to that point in my international career, I was most familiar with what is known as a contribution agreement. One of the differences between these two funding mechanisms is the level of reporting back to the donor. The latter is much more demanding in that regard. In comparison, an American grant requires very little reporting. I was composing weekly missives to IFES headquarters in Washington, DC, but those accounts were not shared with USAID, which was contrary to how I had always functioned in the implementation of projects funded by Canada. IFES met on occasion with USAID representatives in Skopje, essentially to compare notes on how the preparations for the elections were proceeding.

The IFES Field Director (my boss) was an American lawyer with extensive experience in the US in democratic development. Besides me, there were three other international colleagues in the office. They worked on procedural training, communications and logistics. Our office supported regular policy dialogue with the other international bodies and we coached a local non-governmental organization to help them promote the role of Parliament in Macedonia. We all worked with local colleagues who facilitated liaison with national authorities, provided translation and interpretation services, both linguistic and cultural, and supported us in a multitude of other ways necessary to run the office.

A personal accomplishment of which I am proud was that, independently, I founded a successful monthly women's networking breakfast in Skopje. I modelled it on a similar body I had been part of in Ottawa. Professional women gathered once a month at a local hotel to share expertise and experiences over coffee and a light breakfast. It was a satisfying endeavour to link both international and Macedonian women in this way. I like to think it was meaningful for all of us.

Macedonia is just south of Kosovo, so I was not far from friends I had made when I was posted there the year before. It was a two- to three-hour drive back to Mitrovica, where I had lived and worked for six months. I actually took my mother there when she came over to visit. It was quite an experience for her at the age of 74.

In Calgary, where my mother spent her adult life, she had endeared herself to a Kosovar family who had sought refuge in Canada. My mother had helped them with some furniture and various household items so they were very grateful and treated her like the family elder she was to them. Their parents still lived in Kosovo, near Mitrovica, and my mother and I were able to visit them. It was quite an emotional affair and a cross-cultural one too. My mother was particularly taken aback to find the father of this Muslim family simply continuing his regular prayer session in the middle of the living room upon our arrival. Once that was completed, we managed to have a pleasant visit, despite my spotty Serbian, which the Kosovar elders understood easily. What a trooper my mother was to sally forth with me to that conflict-ridden, politically divided town. One of my international friends there was an American police officer, who spent some time with us during that visit. I think my mother felt more comfortable having an armed escort along for the ride!

But I have skipped over a most memorable moment when Mum arrived in Macedonia. Not having my own vehicle, I had asked my landlord if he would take me to meet Mum at the airport. He readily agreed. That evening we set off with just enough time to meet her when she arrived. What I didn't know was that Vlado needed to stop for gas en route. That diversion took a lot longer than I would have liked, and sure enough we were late arriving at the airport. In fact, we were so late that my poor mother was standing waiting outside the airport all by herself! I felt just dreadful but somehow she had managed to feel at ease all on her own in a foreign country in the dark! I do know she was very grateful when we finally showed up, perhaps so much so that she chose not to scold me for my egregious error. Maybe she realized the circumstances had been beyond my control.

138

During the year I spent in Skopje, I traveled overland to Greece on a few occasions as it was not too far, and it was oh so good to reach the sea. I treated Mum to that adventure too. We drove to the city of Thessaloniki en route to Halkidiki, the three peninsulas that stick out into the Aegean Sea in the northeast of the country. This part of northern Greece is known as Macedonia, which is why the Former Yugoslav Republic of Macedonia had previously had such a long official name. Not until June 2018 did Greece and FYROM, as it was known, officially agree to change the name of the latter to the Republic of North Macedonia.

In December 2002, my assignment was winding up after a year and I was to return to Canada with some trepidation, as you can imagine. We had a big farewell party, after which I packed my bags and dragged my sorry soul off to the airport to leave a country yet again, where I had spent a full year. An era of almost six years in the Balkans was coming to a close. I have not returned to Macedonia or Kosovo since then. Previously though, in April 2001 after observing elections in Montenegro, I was able to go for a brief visit to see friends in Mostar in Bosnia. As they say, however, you can never go back. So onward I went to the next adventures awaiting me. I would never have guessed I would become a federal public servant in Ottawa at the ripe young age of almost 54.

17. Re-inventing Myself, Again!

Over the six-year period between 1996 and 2002 I gained a new area of expertise – election administration in post-conflict environments. Just how was this going to translate to a normal job in Canada? I didn't want to work at Elections Canada although I was selected to work during an election as a returning officer in a polling station in Ottawa.

In February 2003, a couple of months after returning to Canada, I had a wonderful opportunity. I learned that the Government of Canada was offering what it called a Job Finding Club. It was a three-week program, five days a week from eight to four o'clock. About 15 of us met daily to learn and practice skills that would land us jobs that matched our experience and qualifications. It was a very useful program.

In 2003, we used the Yellow Pages to research our field of choice! We made 'connecting calls', which were essentially cold calls, but just the name change gave us more confidence to phone strangers to sell our skill sets. One very important thing we learned was to avoid leaving voice-mail messages. If you do so, you give away your power. Instead, we were told to continue calling, choosing different times of the day to reach the person we wanted. Once connected, we asked for information meetings to help us expand our networks, and we honoured our requests to have short, ten-minute sessions with those who agreed to meet us. We shared challenges and successes with fellow course participants. We wrote down and read aloud messages of daily gratitude. In the years since then, I have passed on these useful tips to those trying to get into the field of international development, or any career for that matter.

I already knew I was skilled in finding interesting international opportunities. I just had to transcribe them to domestic settings. I made progress. Through determined networking, I managed to get selected for a temporary, part-time position in the international section of the Canadian Nurses Association (CNA). It was a small team of women with a wonderful director, Dr. June Webber, who is now a vice-president at St. Francis Xavier University in Antigonish, Nova Scotia. As a generalist, I loved the chance to work closely with nurses and learn about their field of work, even though I was in an administrative role. One of the most interesting tasks was to manage a visit of many nurses from several countries and continents for an international conference being held in Ottawa. I loved getting to know these dedicated caregivers and seeing their global solidarity to improve health conditions in their home countries. I also learned a lot about health issues around the world.

At the same time that I was working with the CNA in Ottawa, I applied my enhanced skills in finding local assignments. Another great result from these efforts was getting two consulting jobs with the Canadian International Development Agency (CIDA) by reconnecting with a woman I had worked with on another consulting assignment in the private sector.

So, I had the proverbial foot in the door at CIDA and when two positions were posted on the internet for a 48-hour period, I applied. Just as my time with the CNA was drawing to a close later in 2003, CIDA offered me one of these positions, sight unseen – me, that is – in what was called Partnership Branch. I was to work on the Universities and Colleges Program. What a great fit! I started on December 8, 2003, three weeks short of my 54th birthday. I was lucky enough to have another great boss, Ray Woltman, who angelically showed me the ropes of the federal public service in Ottawa.

I hasten to mention however that Dr. Webber at the CNA was not about to let me go just like that. The CNA had just been granted $5 million to implement a project over five years to work on HIV/AIDS in southern Africa, and I was being offered the chance to manage it from Ottawa. Now that was a difficult choice, given how much I had liked working with the CNA. I weighed the pros and cons of each offer. The CNA was a known entity but where would I be after five years? Plus I felt it was unfair for me, who was not a nurse myself, to take on this project working with nurses in southern Africa.

CIDA, on the other hand, had longer employment opportunities although I was initially just being offered a three-month term position. However, I knew that I would have the chance to work in many sectors, not just health, if I were to choose the Canadian government job. I negotiated a starting salary equivalent to what I was making as a consultant and made the decision to work with CIDA.

The irony of the salary negotiation was that I was never able to advance beyond the employment classification I was given at the outset. Furthermore, since I was at the top salary level, in 12.5 years I only got a cost-of-living increase and any increments negotiated by the Public Service Alliance of Canada (PSAC). In retrospect, you might think I should have chosen the position with the CNA but I never regretted joining CIDA as it gave me many interesting initiatives that suited me very well. By now, you have probably understood that, at all costs, I would avoid getting stuck in a rut!

18. Being a Federal Public Servant in Ottawa

A few weeks shy of my 54th birthday, I started my new career as a federal public servant with the Canadian International Development Agency (CIDA) in Ottawa. In some ways it was like coming full circle.

Allow me to recap. I had begun my professional life in 1974, almost 30 years earlier, as a teacher in Dawson City, Yukon where I was a territorial public servant for two years. Then I went rogue, working as a volunteer teacher for a year in the even smaller Yukon community of Carcross. This break with convention continued as I cycled from Vancouver to San Francisco on my way to Australia, to get a cheaper airfare! On my working holiday visa for a year, I taught for about eight months in a boys' technical school outside of Melbourne. Then I was set free again as I traveled for four months in New Zealand, plus a couple more months in Oz. Next was South East Asia, beginning in Bali for three weeks, with my now-beloved bicycle!

That bicycle flew seven more flights to capital cities in Asia over a three-month period. In Canada two years after leaving Vancouver for Australia, I settled down to teach English as a Second Language in Calgary for eight years, followed by a year and a half in Ethiopia as a volunteer teacher. The Ethiopia experience was the catalyst for a career change to international development, which meant a move across the country to be close to the 'trough' in Ottawa. The non-governmental organizations there picked me up quickly and I stayed with two of them for seven years until I broke away again, for six years of election administration in three countries in the Balkans. Wishing to lead a more normal life in Ottawa, I landed in the relatively secure environment of the federal public service.

Little did I know quite how precarious my employment there would be. It was not uncommon in the early 2000s for public servants to take early retirement at 55 after putting in some 25 or 30 years with the government. As usual, I was on the road less traveled, at least age-wise in this case, as I was just a year younger than those ending their careers and I was just starting afresh!

In the Universities and Colleges Program where I first landed in 'officialdom', the Canadian government provided funding for Canada's post-secondary institutions to develop and implement education projects in developing countries. As a senior program officer, I analyzed proposals, monitored project progress and liaised with the stakeholders. I covered those institutions in Western Canada, my original home turf having been Alberta. This suited me well and I learned the subtleties of working in a federal government office.

I was hired on a three-month term which meant I had very little job security. Fortunately, I was able to prove my worth and was soon awarded a year-long term. Near the end of that time, I competed for an indeterminate position – such an unfortunate phrase but coveted because that's what it took to become a permanent public servant. Despite good performance assessments, I misinterpreted one of the two essential questions on the written exam and was not successful. I remember being terribly demoralized and decided to go where I might be better appreciated.

A new team was being formed in CIDA at that time. By now, it was 2005 and Canada's politicians saw the need to create a Canadian equivalent of the American Peace Corps. The terminology was that Canada wanted to get 'boots on the ground', and so Canada Corps was born. One of the sections in this new mechanism was the Mobilization and Democracy team, or MAD as we affectionately called ourselves. I cannot remember our official mission statement but, essentially, our job was to deploy Canadians to observe elections in developing countries. This mission was right up my alley, having worked on eight elections in the Balkans. The Canada Corps directors recruited me without hesitation, as I had the type of field experience they needed. I was back in my element.

The MAD team oversaw the recruitment of Canadians to observe elections in developing countries. Haiti was one such example but our biggest project was to create an independent Canadian election observation mission for the 2006 parliamentary elections in the West Bank and Gaza. We selected a head of mission, a core team and both long- and short-term observers. To implement this, we set up an office in Ramallah in the West Bank. I joined another colleague out on the ground for a month during the implementation of this initiative. It was all consuming, creating an intense learning environment, not only from a technical point of view but also because we were in a complex geo-political and historical setting.

I had always found the situation in the Middle East to be very complicated and equally disturbing, so I had not followed events there closely. In some ways it was a good thing because it resulted in greater neutrality, which is essential in working in the political sphere of another country. I was however aware of the suicide bombings that took place there on occasion. I distinctly remember how vulnerable I felt the first time I was in an ordinary car on a busy street in Jerusalem. Pulling up alongside a local bus, I couldn't help thinking there might be a suicide bomber nearby, perhaps even on the bus. It was both humbling and terrifying at the same time.

I have always wondered what could be so wrong within a society that a mother is proud to have her son selected to carry out a suicide attack. During the month that I was there, I began to see beyond the tip of that iceberg. Even though there was no outright violence, there was the ever-present antagonism against the Palestinians who did not have normal freedom of movement. Being subjected to control points to go from A to B on a regular basis was a passive form of psychological warfare. Instead of taking half an hour to get to work, it could easily take twice that long, in both directions, to go from one control point to another. As a foreigner with a diplomatic passport, I was exempt from passing through these checkpoints but if we had local staff with us, we would have to wait for them to pass through the controls. It helped me understand what caused the simmering violence which could easily bubble over.

I look back on that mission with some amazement. For example, I was allowed to drive a rented car in Ramallah. I never traveled alone but it was quite a feat to drive in what looked like total chaos. I still have a vivid picture of the police traffic control officer who stood in the middle of the mayhem with his whistle and white gloves on his flailing arms that directed the traffic. As I sat behind the steering wheel, Lee Nickerson, a lieutenant colonel in the Canadian Forces, coached me on the rules of the road. He stressed the importance of making eye contact with anyone I was moving around or past, be it a pedestrian risking their life or the driver of another vehicle. Lee had previously been posted to the Golan Heights so he knew the territories. On a rare day off, we ventured up to his former workstation overlooking the terrain. We passed through Israel and got a taste of a certain lack of courtesy there. From the high point of land, we could see a signpost indicating Damascus which was not far away in neighbouring Syria.

The actual election day did not disappoint in terms of its historic impact on the region. As it happened, I was assigned to the Israeli Ministry of Foreign Affairs in Jerusalem for the day. Although I was disappointed to be inside during the voting, it turned out that it was intriguing to see how the senior Israeli officials functioned that day.

Not unlike Canada's Department of Foreign Affairs, the Israeli Ministry was in a modern, well-appointed building for bureaucrats. Interestingly, its high-tech equipment was much more sophisticated than I had seen in Canada. On a huge screen we were able to watch what was happening at various polling stations in the territories of the West Bank which appeared relatively calm. Of course, the language used was Hebrew which I do not understand so no doubt I missed many things. Those present treated me well and very respectfully.

The day went surprisingly smoothly. Our observers and other international teams declared it a free and fair election. However, the successful party was Hamas, which is considered a terrorist organization. As a result, developed countries withdrew their aid from the region, a most unfortunate move, given the high degree of need. Hamas had run a solid campaign but no one, not even Hamas, expected it would win. Its error was not to have created a political wing for the purposes of the election as the IRA had done in Ireland with Sinn Fein. It was a very tough way for Hamas to learn a lesson.

One thing I found odd during my month in the region was that Canada's senior representative to the West Bank and Gaza was not aware the Ministry of

Foreign Affairs was based in Jerusalem. For him, Canada's counterparts in Israel were based in Tel Aviv. I found this hard to comprehend but I was still a toddler in this business, with just over two years under my belt with CIDA at that point. I was in no position to engage Canada's representative to explain the situation. It remains a curiosity to me to this day.

I realize now that I must have been granted another extension to my determinate status, perhaps when I joined Canada Corps. That timing no longer seemed relevant. What mattered was that I could apply for a permanent position at my level and compete for my own job. I passed the first step of the competition, the written exam. Phew! Next, I was interviewed by my then-bosses. I thought it went fine. Wrong. I was to find out I had not succeeded. This time I was devastated and mortified beyond words. I could scarcely look anyone in the eye. As soon as I could, I fled! I relied on those good old networking skills of mine and in no time found myself another position in the Agency. What a relief!

The Canada Fund for Africa (CFA) welcomed me with open arms and I was extremely grateful to find myself in their midst. One of my new bosses had been similarly embarrassed by her lack of success to move up the ranks, so she could understand my pain. It was 2006 and I felt at home again, as I had in my two other positions, even though they had not lasted long. The important thing was that I had interesting work. The CFA had been granted $500 million during a G8 Summit meeting in Kananaskis in 2002, so we had lots of 'do-re-mi' to fund deserving initiatives.

I became responsible for some interesting projects with a Pan-African focus, which meant they were multi-country. One project concerned youth and HIV/AIDS in two English-speaking countries, Ethiopia and Kenya, and in two French-speaking countries, which I cannot recall now. I was able to visit the other two and I so appreciated being able to return to the two countries I already knew. The other interesting aspect of the project was that it was managed by a coalition of four NGOs: Save the Children, World Vision, Care Canada and Plan International. It was refreshing to see these organizations working together to meet targets instead of having to compete against each other for Canadian government funding.

Other worthwhile projects I oversaw were the West Africa Police Project and the Kofi Annan Peacekeeping Centre in Ghana. The implementing partner for those two projects was the Pearson Peacekeeping Centre in Ottawa. These projects were again right up my alley as I had worked with international police in the Balkans, where we were also peacekeeping. I found it intriguing to work alongside police officers and learn about the culture of that occupation.

Once when I was in Accra, Ghana monitoring the two projects, I met up by chance with Dr. June Webber, whom you may recall was my boss at the Canadian Nurses Association. I was in the lobby of the Tulip Hotel when she walked in. We looked at each other in disbelief and asked what the other was doing in Ghana. She was part of the African tour of Canada's then-Governor General, Michaëlle Jean! That evening was their last in Ghana and they were having an informal dinner out by the hotel pool. June had been told she could invite a friend and she had thought, "Yeah, right! Where would I find that friend?" And *voilà*, there I was, most happy to oblige and join the party.

The GG looked terrific in Ghanaian dress in the colours of the country's flag – red, yellow and green. I had a chance to speak with her and I remember the conversation was rich. It touched on foreign languages, a topic dear to my heart. Another memorable element of the evening was realizing that Ryan Hreljac of Ryan's Well Foundation was a member of the GG's tour. During my time with the Canadian Nurses Association, I heard Ryan speak at an international health conference in Ottawa. He was 12 years old at the time, and the delivery of his speech was as polished as any adult professional. As a former teacher, I was overwhelmed by the capabilities of this young fellow. I remember afterwards going to talk to his mother and telling her how impressed I was. It was quite a coincidence to run into him again on another continent some three years later.

Another country I visited in West Africa was Guinea Bissau, which was holding a multi-country, multi-day meeting on the topic of the disarmament of small arms. I oversaw Canada's role in a United Nations project to reduce the number of small arms in the region. The initiative was drawing to a close but I found it fascinating to get a glimpse of its tail end. Representatives were present from The Gambia and Senegal. Three languages were spoken – English, French and Portuguese. Incorporating three languages was much more difficult than Canada's efforts to function in just two official languages at the federal level.

Another project I followed was with the Economic Community of West African States (ECOWAS). This umbrella body had its headquarters in Abuja, the capital city of Nigeria. I traveled there several times for project steering committee meetings. This project was the most challenging, due to its political nature. For that reason, CIDA (i.e., me in this case) worked with Canada's Department of Foreign Affairs to push the project forward. Having these two Canadian government bodies work side by side was an accomplishment, due to our inherently different cultures. I have always been a big supporter of teamwork – we all have strengths to bring to the table. Nevertheless, the cohesion on the West African side was yet another challenge. Although I can't remember the details of the issues that stood in the way, I do know they were related to lack of progress in the implementation of the project objectives. They appeared almost insurmountable but we kept at it. Hopefully the project had some long-term results that were worth the money and time invested.

This lack of clarity may be related to the fact I was again getting ready to move to another program at CIDA. As if West Africa had not been exciting enough, something much bigger was on the horizon.

Before moving on, it is important to note that after three years in a determinate position at CIDA, I finally got that coveted indeterminate status while I was working on the CFA program. It was germane in terms of what was to follow.

19. First Posting with the Government of Canada

Part of the allure of working for CIDA was the possibility of being posted overseas to a developing country. Now that I was an indeterminate federal public servant, I had become eligible to apply for a posting. My chances were minimal, given that I had only three years' experience with the Feds. Nevertheless, I would apply, not being one to shrink away from a challenge. I can't recall how many times I tried before I succeeded, but I distinctly remember that last effort when I was selected!

Postings usually take place in August but the selection process begins as early as January. Each country program holds an information session about its work and the positions in the field. Interested candidates are encouraged to attend so as to make informed decisions. I remember hearing about the opportunity in South Sudan and so I attended its information session. Although it was interesting, I realized the physical setting would be similar to where I had been in Ethiopia some 20 years previously. That made it less appealing but the final deterrent was the fact that Canadians working there were the only nationality that did not qualify for any kind of special R&R package (rest and recreation) while all other participating nationalities got regular, well-earned breaks. It was relatively easy to rule it out for that reason alone, given that it was an especially tough posting.

For what program would I have the best chances of being selected? Presumably to the countries considered less desirable. So, you guessed it: I attended the information session for Afghanistan. It is perhaps a little difficult to tell you why, but I was

155

pumped after attending that session, probably because it had been five years since I had returned from my six-year stint in the Balkans. Life in Ottawa was becoming pretty comfortable. Why then would I not want to stay there? Well, I put it down to my fear of getting stuck in a rut, pure and simple.

So I applied for the Afghanistan program and was selected. There were two possible locations in Afghanistan – the embassy in Kabul or Canada's military camp in Kandahar. The former interested me more, but of course it was not what I was offered. After all, why would those making the decisions overlook my six years in post-conflict places like Bosnia, Kosovo and Macedonia? I have to admit I was an obvious fit for Kandahar. I went to more information sessions to learn just what I would be getting myself into and I got hooked. I remember being very excited at the thought of the journey ahead. It turned out to be the first of three postings as a federal public servant.

I had already informed my parents I was applying to be part of one of Canada's embassies. My mother was particularly pleased with this idea. She asked me excitedly, "Karen, do you think you might be sent to, you know, some place like Paris or London?" Ah dear Mum, how hard to have to remind her that France and the UK were not exactly in need of development assistance. When the choice was made and I had to break the news that I was going to a war-torn country yet again, it was particularly tough for all of us.

My parents were divorced when I was 21 but some 37 years later, they were still on good terms. I phoned my father first, because I hoped he could keep my mother calm. When I told him I was being sent to Kandahar, he asked hesitantly, "Is that the place where there is more fighting?" I had to be honest and say yes. I assured him I would be safe in the confines of Canada's military camp. He had long ago learned there was no point in trying to convince me to change my mind on big decisions like these so he was supportive and helped me break the news to my mother. My poor Mum had no say in the matter when it came down to it.

One thing that made the decision easier was that I was not going alone to Kandahar. As half a dozen of us prepared for this hardship posting, we got to know each other very well. One colleague was half my age (58 at the time) but we bonded and I knew I would have someone in whom I could confide during the tough times that were inevitably going to come.

Our first test was to participate in a ten-day simulation exercise in Wainwright, Alberta where the Canadian Forces (CF) had created a mock camp. It was late May and not very warm. We slept on cots in big tents and used ablution blocks as we would in the field. We trained with our CF colleagues who would be there when we were. Many of them were with CIMIC, which stands for civilian military cooperation. Scenarios were acted out on a daily basis, with Afghan immigrants to Canada playing the role of their countrymen and women, although admittedly they were mostly men.

We had drills in the middle of the night when we had to seek refuge in bunkers. We handled firearms and rode in military vehicles. Yes, this was going to be one big adventure. With us on this exercise were our civilian colleagues from Foreign Affairs who would also be deployed to Canada's military base. It was an excellent training ground and we got to know each other in a way unprecedented in posting exercises.

Before we were considered ready to post to such a tough place, we were required to attend Hazardous Environment Training (HET) at the Royal Military College of Canada in Kingston, Ontario. The HET was a five-day program where we lived on site and attended theoretical classes and participated in outdoor exercises. Most important of all was the mock kidnapping experience we underwent. I have never written much about this as we were asked not to. Suffice it to say, it was my least favourite part of the training but I was aware of how important it was. So much so, that I was to attend another two sessions of the HET in the next four or five years due to further postings in conflict zones.

I would venture to say few people would describe the military as creative but I can assure you, I learned firsthand about their ability to fabricate realistic scenarios in order to prepare the forces and the civilians for challenging environments.

These preparations are not normally part of getting ready to go on a posting. One requirement we did have in common with our colleagues being posted to less dangerous parts of the world was a visit to Health Canada. We had to be deemed physically and mentally fit enough to represent Canada abroad. Some of us were worried we would not pass muster as we had heard stories of others being prevented from going overseas because of a health concern.

I was anxious about my fate as I waited to see the doctor at Health Canada. There I was waiting in one of those paper hospital robes that already erode your dignity, when in walked the person who was to make this big decision for me. My first reaction was relief because the white-coated doctor who presented himself had salt and pepper hair! Phew! That meant he was less likely to discriminate against me because of my age (58). Instead, his opening remarks broke the ice right away, "You're going to Afghanistan, right? And so just who the hell did you piss off?!" I've got a lot of mileage out of that story. My dad, in particular, got a great kick out of it and often asked me to repeat it to amuse people.

I passed Health Canada's examination. I could now begin the usual preparations, like deciding what to do with my house, car, and various other possessions. Going to Kandahar meant I could only take the bare minimum with me. Should the camp be evacuated at any time, we would be allowed to take only a minimal amount of gear with us. That was a challenge, getting it down to the basics, as we would be gone for at least a year which was almost twice as long as our military colleagues. The other consideration was that as women, we had to choose clothing that was culturally acceptable. For example, our derrieres should be covered by long tunics, our ankles were not to show and we would have to cover our heads in the presence of Afghan men.

On top of that there was the mental and emotional preparation for such a journey. I remember well going for a walk along the Rideau Canal with one of my best pals, Lt. Col. Doug Cargo. Ironically, he was envious of my posting, which was not being offered to him although I'm not sure why, nor do I know how the Canadian military recruitment for Afghanistan was organized. Anyway, that evening, I was feeling anxious and even weepy. I admitted to Doug I was scared. I recognized there was a chance I might not make it home alive. Doug heard me out and somehow managed to soothe my battered soul. I was extremely grateful for his friendship during that difficult time.

Finally, I was ready to leave in July 2008. En route, I stopped first in Sri Lanka to visit a friend working there. It didn't work out very well though as there was a high-level summit meeting a few days after my arrival and this meant the airport would be closed.

I thought I had better get out of Dodge quickly so I could report for duty on time.

Dubai was my next port of call. At that time, it was the jumping off place to get to Kandahar. I was fortunate to be introduced to Canadian friends of my brother Liam. They were living there in a lovely three-bedroom, three-bathroom apartment in a gated community, complete with swimming pool, which was most welcome in that heat. I stopped there for a few days and then managed to execute the military meet-up at the Dubai airport. This was the mechanism to get out to the multi-national military camp in the desert, the location of which I was not to know. Once at the camp, I would be flown in a DC-3 military plane into Kandahar, along with our soldiers and any other Canadian civilians en route. But before departing for theatre, I was kitted out for civilian military duty. The combat equipment consisted of a flak jacket that probably weighed at least forty pounds, a helmet, gloves as I recall, and special impact resistant, wrap-around glasses to protect my eyes in the case of an explosion, and from what I was soon to learn was the ubiquitous dust.

It was July, which meant that it was extremely hot – sometimes up to 50 degrees Celsius! And in all that protective clothing! Oh my, I felt like a baked potato wrapped in foil on the barbeque! On arrival at the Kandahar Airfield, I was met by a civilian who took me right away to get my ID card. It was an essential tool to get around safely on the camp, which had some 12,000 personnel of many nationalities!

ID cards usually have photos on them, right? But I had just taken a flight of at least three hours and I was wearing many pounds of protective gear. How could I possibly have my photo taken? Well, I learned that even if you feel a mess, it is possible not to look like one! I was astonished to see my mug shot was not bad, given the adverse circumstances. Oddly enough it is a life lesson I carry with me in difficult times – how I feel on the inside is not necessarily what shows on the outside.

20. Kandahar, Afghanistan

How am I **going to describe** such an unusual experience as living on a Canadian military base in Kandahar, Afghanistan for a full year, during which, halfway through, I turned 59? I suppose I could say I survived, even though it is obvious as I sit here over a decade later to tell this part of my life story.

I have already described the journey to Kandahar City in the southern desert province of the same name in Afghanistan in late July 2008. The military DC-3 that brought me from the United Arab Emirates landed at the Kandahar Airfield, otherwise known as KAF, the multi-national operational military base for the southern region of the country. Senior Canadian officers strategized there with their counterparts from other countries stationed in the region – the British, the Dutch and the Americans, to name a few. This was the pulse of the counterterrorist action centre.

I was not to spend the majority of my time at KAF, although a handful of my civilian colleagues were based there. It was the hub as we transited in and out of 'theatre', as it was known. For this reason, I do not have the right background to provide details of everything that went on there. I can tell you though what KAF did offer to those of us going into Kandahar City itself. You have probably heard on the grapevine that there was a Tim Horton's selling coffee and donuts to the 12,000 residents of KAF. Another facility was a sports field for field hockey; this area was surrounded by merchants selling local wares and offering such services as massage, esthetics and haircuts. We enjoyed well-equipped gyms, huge cafeterias with varied cuisines and fortunately, other colleagues with whom we could debrief in person.

163

These were all welcome attractions after being stationed for up to eight weeks at a time at the much smaller military camp where I was headed.

Sleeping quarters at KAF were in basic shipping containers that provided the bare minimum. The whole airfield was a dry zone, i.e., no alcohol was allowed, and there was a strict no-fraternization policy, which meant no intimacy at all. Residents worked long hard hours. It is important to mention the R&R (rest and recreation) policy, which varied among the donor countries according to whether you were civilian, police or military. For Canadian civilians like me it was a requirement to leave theatre every eight weeks to the day, not a day earlier, and not a day later. We planned our own getaways and made all the necessary travel arrangements, although trips involving the military getting us to and from Dubai were beyond our control. This meant adding to an already demanding workload but it was still a welcome diversion to make these plans. Most generous of all was that we were given very healthy budgets for these forays and although we had to account for our expenditures, we recognized how fortunate we were. My trips were to Greece, Canada, Mauritius, Egypt, Italy, and China in the year I was posted to Kandahar. We had two weeks from the time we left the camp until we returned to it.

I cannot recall how long I was at KAF before being transported to the military camp where I would be based for a year. I think it was only a day or two before I was loaded into a military tank known as a LAV (light armoured vehicle). We could see nothing outside the vehicle except via a camera screen inside the cavity in which we rode. It was perhaps just as well. In the depths of the dry July heat with temperatures soaring above 50 degrees Celsius, the flat terrain over which we were riding was an unattractive expanse of brown dust, as thick as sand on a beach, but nowhere near as pleasant.

Nonetheless, it was exciting to finally arrive at the camp. It was one of several provincial reconstruction teams, or PRTs, spread around the country. Canada's PRT in Kandahar was known as Camp Nathan Smith. Smith was a private with the Princess Patricia's Canadian Light Infantry; he was accidentally killed by an American fighter jet during a military exercise in Afghanistan in 2002. The camp named after him was the site of a former fruit canning factory modified to house a military contingent.

On my arrival in July 2008, there were about 350 Canadian troops at the camp, about 50 Canadian civilians and a dozen or so American soldiers. As a civilian, I was lodged in a shipping container that measured 20ft. x 8ft. It had two windows, an air-conditioner/heater unit, a single bed, and a minimal closet/cupboard. I was on the second floor alongside and across from ten similar units. I was lucky to have a container to myself, perhaps because I was the oldest civilian in the camp. I was very grateful to have my own private space, no matter how basic it was. The women's ablution block was about 150 meters away. Due to middle-of-the-night forays to this essential facility, I always knew what phase the moon was in! And I will say that the rugged Kandahar hills in the distance looked particularly lovely under the bright starry skies.

During my stay at the PRT, our military provided pretty much everything I needed. I ate all my meals in the mess hall at set times. I had access to the basic gym. Naturally there was also a field hockey rink but that was not my cup of tea. I could walk for exercise inside the perimeter of the camp. One lap was about 700 metres. We were also extremely lucky to have a reservoir for fire-fighting purposes which could also be used for swimming. It was round, about 30 feet across and maybe five feet deep.

Given the horrifically high temperatures in the summer, this was a godsend. It is where I got my morning exercise before breakfast, at least until the camp sergeant major decided I should not be allowed to swim there alone. Fortunately, I was able to recruit my neighbour, Lisa, who graciously agreed to come and supervise my exercise while she read and enjoyed her morning coffee. It suited me to a tee because prior to that I was not entirely on my own. In fact, a male Afghan employee was cleaning the facilities in the reservoir enclosure. That was perhaps what made it a bit unsafe for me, a Western woman clad only in a bathing suit and showering and dressing there afterwards. To be honest, it was a bit creepy. Needless to say, I was very happy to have Lisa there.

Since this luxury was not technically a pool, there was no ladder in or out. The former was no problem but I did have trouble getting out, so I went to the supply officer to ask for a bucket and a rope. Now, as you can imagine, these materials are not normally requested, and understandably this could cause concern. I had to explain what I wanted to do with them.

I tied the rope to the handle of the bucket and when it was time to get out of the water, I dropped the bucket into the water, turned it upside down and left the rope up on the side. Then I could stand on the bucket to get out more easily and pull the bucket out of the water. I did eventually get to the stage when I was strong enough to pull myself out without this improvised tool.

The camp also had a small PX, a first aid station. and a military chaplain. I attended far too many memorial services for our fallen soldiers. Those were the toughest of times. Too many of our young soldiers were killed by improvised explosive devices (IEDs) while outside the wire, i.e., the relative safety of the camp. I never got used to those occasions. The first one, less than a couple of weeks after my arrival, was particularly difficult. I left with my eyes downcast and my face moist from my tears. What was the appropriate follow-up? There were no easy answers.

The camaraderie in the camp was exemplary. As we all ate our meals together, we got to know each other well and enjoyed the healthy mix of diverse organizational cultures. The civilians came from Foreign Affairs, the Canadian International Development Agency and Corrections Canada. The police were members of the RCMP as well as provincial and local police services. As for the military, the air force, the army and the navy were all represented. We learned a lot about each other as we shared this intense experience.

One of our evening diversions was playing euchre, a game I didn't know although it was similar to bridge. I had taken several hours of bridge lessons in Ottawa before I knew I would be spending the next year in a conflict zone. Unfortunately, no one at the camp played bridge so I learned euchre and discovered how much easier it is and how much fun it can be.

Another opportunity to chill at the camp was affectionately known as a 'beer call'. Like KAF, the PRT was a dry camp and had the same rule that fraternization was not allowed. For the former, it was obvious that none of us could afford to be inebriated in the case of an attack. As for the latter, we were aware that fraternizing in such a volatile environment might not be a good idea either so having a beer call every six weeks or so was appealing, especially in the unyielding summer heat. Rumours that a call was imminent were met with great interest. Often it was not confirmed until a few hours before. It usually took place at the same time as a BBQ. We could each have two beers or if you preferred wine, you had to find a pal to share a bottle. You really appreciate indulging when it happens so seldom.

Christmas 2008 at the PRT was a collaborative affair. Our colleague from Correctional Services Canada dressed up as Santa Claus. I wonder now who had thought to bring a Santa suit to the camp, although I have a good hunch it was our military! The civilians participated in a secret Santa gift exchange that made us all laugh at what we had managed to scrounge up as gifts. Dinner that evening in the mess hall was an elaborate affair with all the traditional trimmings of the season. We were safe, our bellies were full and some of us were 'living the dream', a term most often used by our police colleagues. We hoped we were making a difference while at the same time we were certainly having the time of our lives.

The camp had a helicopter landing pad which was often how I traveled to and from the camp. One such occasion took place during a particularly difficult time when the camp was being evacuated due to an expected attack. This was about halfway through my year there and fortunately it was the only time it was necessary to move us to safer ground.

We had just a few hours to gather our gear for a few days away from the camp over at KAF. In my case, it was just before I was scheduled to go on R&R, which meant I had to pack in a real hurry for my two weeks away. It was always an effort to extract myself from work and life at the camp so I was the last person to get onto the large Chinook helicopter as it took off. It is not easy to move quickly wearing the heavy protective gear, plus I had luggage for a two-week holiday. The chopper was literally lifting off the ground as I crawled onto its open ramp at the back. Then I had to continue scrambling on all fours, with my luggage, forward into the body of the chopper to avoid being sucked out the back of it. That got the old heart pumping big time!

On another occasion going in the opposite direction, i.e., from KAF to the PRT, I was in the much smaller Blackhawk helicopter. Someone took a photo of me sitting inside the chopper as we waited to take off. I had on my protective gear – the flak jacket, the helmet and the impact resistant wrap-around glasses – and I was grinning from ear to ear. When I saw that image, it was hard not to recognize myself as the adrenaline junky I undoubtedly was at that time. It is not easy to explain but there it was, captured clearly for me to see and accept, that look of pure joy all over my face!

Yet there were very tough times. The most personal occurred on April 1st, ironic given that it was April Fool's Day. I was in a meeting in my director's office at the camp at mid-day when we heard a thunderous explosion. It was not at our camp but farther away in the city. At the time we didn't know what the target had been.

A couple of hours later, after lunch, the young Afghan man who worked closely with me came into my office and sat beside my desk. He said, "Sometimes I hate my country." I asked what was wrong. He explained that the provincial council chambers had been the target of a large suicide bomb attack. Several Afghan government officials had been spending the day there in a training session. One of them was the provincial director of education who we dealt with on a regular basis. He had been killed and so had the provincial deputy director of health. What appeared to bother my Afghan colleague most was that the education director had just been out of the country for

169

a short break and had not yet been able to go to the neighbouring province to see his wife and family before the attack. It was a tragic loss. The director had been a good man and we were working well with him in our effort to build more schools to increase the access to education for all children, girls included.

It was not long after this incident that I was at KAF on my way out of the country for an R&R. I got a frantic call from an Afghan–American woman who worked with us. She was sobbing so I knew something horrific must have happened but I could not figure out what. She was so distraught I couldn't understand what she was saying. I was trying to determine who had been hurt or killed. Perhaps it was one of her family members although I kept thinking it might be one of the Afghan women we knew. We had one female assistant who took a big risk by simply coming to the PRT on a daily basis. Or, it could have been the provincial director of women's affairs. Her predecessor had been assassinated as she left her home one morning to go to work.

Eventually I learned it was neither of these women. Instead, it was one of the female members of the provincial council. She had been shot down on her way home after a council meeting that day. It had just happened 45 minutes earlier. Rangina was convinced the traditional pale blue burqa the councilor had been wearing had contributed to the brutal death. The burqa has only a narrow netting over the eyes so the victim would not realize she was about to be attacked. Rangina was inconsolable. All I could do was let her pour out her grief.

These incidents within two weeks of each other were taking their toll on me as well. It was lucky I was on my way out of the country. A Canadian colleague at KAF recognized my malaise over these tragedies and suggested I see a counsellor at KAF. I agreed, needing little persuasion. She helped me make an appointment and I saw a military colleague, a captain.

In the waiting room, I filled out a form to explain the reason for my visit. I realized the questions were geared for soldiers not civilians, as I was being asked if there was a chance that I wanted to hurt myself or perhaps others. After the first 20 minutes or so with the counsellor, she told me she didn't understand why I was there to see her. I told her I just needed to go somewhere to cry. She agreed this would be helpful but understood there was nowhere I could do this without attracting unwanted attention. In the end I shed some tears in her office and she helped by reminding me it would be abnormal if I felt no emotion at all over these losses. She talked about the grieving process and the need to let it happen in its own time. It was good preparation for my R&R – what timing!

I have mentioned I was working on our education files. Building schools in Kandahar was considered a Signature Project, which was one of three the Government of Canada was promoting to the Canadian public about our investment in development in Afghanistan. We wanted to improve access to education, to improve the quality of education by training more teachers, especially women, and to create opportunities for women and girls. I can't tell you how many times we reported on the number of schools constructed, or how often we had to count the number of teachers trained under our programming.

At the PRT, I was the go-to person for gender equality matters, which is a cross-cutting theme in all of Canada's assistance to developing countries. One initiative I launched with the help of the Afghan team was to create an opportunity for women to sell their wares at the weekly market held just beside our camp. To allow this to take place, we had to negotiate with the men who were the usual vendors. Surprisingly they were willing to give up one week every three months or so for the women to be the sole vendors. It was the culture of the country that prohibited women and men from being together in public in that way.

It was quite an accomplishment to work out this compromise and allow the women to develop the skills required to make the day profitable for them. I learned some of them did not even have basic numeracy skills. It was quite sobering really. But everyone cooperated to create this special event. I am pleased to say the practice endured at least a couple of years into 2010. Beyond that I am not sure, as the camp was eventually turned over to the Americans in mid-2011 when the Canadian troops withdrew from Kandahar.

The civilians and the military worked closely together in Kandahar, sharing our expertise and enriching each other with our organizational cultures. It was natural for development workers such as me to collaborate with the team known as CIMIC (Civilian Military Cooperation); we had been exposed to this during our training in Wainwright, Alberta.

On one occasion, CIMIC and I attended a women's focus group with local Kandahari women at our military base. After a two-hour conversation on a broad range of topics relevant to all the women present, we noticed the Afghan women were more relaxed.

During a question-and-answer session, one of the older women asked a very difficult question, "Why is it that with all your resources and all your military might, you have not been able to defeat the Taliban?"

Wow, how do you answer such a question? Fortunately for me, a Canadian military captain spoke up. She said, "It is because the Taliban is among you and we do not want to eliminate innocent individuals in our effort to get rid of the Taliban." I found that to be a very appropriate reply, and one I wouldn't have thought of.

On another occasion, a Canadian CIMIC officer and I met at our camp with an Afghan elder from a nearby village. I don't remember now the purpose of the meeting but what I do remember was an exchange at the end of the meeting through an interpreter, a young Afghan man on contract with the Canadians.

The Afghan elder turned to address me, a Western woman, with my head respectfully covered by a scarf. He said something along these lines, "Madam, I can see you are of an age where you could be comfortably at home in Canada with your grandchildren. However, I see that is not the case. Instead, you are here in my country trying to help improve our situation here. I would like you to know that I recognize your sacrifice and I appreciate it."

Oh my goodness, his thoughtful remarks had quite an impact on me. I struggled to hold back the tears. I was so touched by his will to communicate these sentiments, even though I was vain enough to be concerned he could tell I was old enough to be a grandmother!

Here are a couple of other examples of my reality during the time in Kandahar. Even though I was overseeing a program to build schools there, I was not able to visit the schools to monitor the progress. This was because I would have had to go in a military convoy which would brand the school as associated with the infidels, us, the Canadian 'occupiers'. Instead my Afghan colleague had to monitor the construction process. I also learned about the progress through regular meetings with the provincial director of education. In my mind, this was really the right approach anyway as it helped put the responsibility for the progress in the hands of the Afghans. After all, they were the ultimate beneficiaries.

The other example took place near the end of my one-year assignment. I had to attend a multinational and multiagency meeting with the provincial director of education at his office in Kandahar City. It took three military tanks and 18 soldiers to take me to that meeting. En route in the armoured vehicle, I told the soldier beside me that I recognized what my military colleagues were doing for me by taking me there. He smiled, pleased I was aware of this fact, and said, "Just make sure it's a good meeting!"

One of the reasons I had been interested in going to Afghanistan was to see for myself if it was possible to implement development initiatives in such an insecure environment. In my 12 months in Kandahar, I felt it was possible to make some progress. I base this partially on the statistics available at the time. When the Taliban fell in 2001, the number of children in schools was reportedly only 700,000 and very few of them were girls. By 2009, the Afghan Ministry of Education reported there were eight million children in school and almost a third of them were girls. That is more than a ten-fold increase, a feat that would be remarkable in a developed country, not to mention war-torn Afghanistan.

As I have mentioned, it was worrying for my parents to have me working in Afghanistan. I remember a particularly touching phone call with my mother. She started by saying she wanted to ask a difficult question and she hoped it would not make me mad. I encouraged her to go ahead.

"Well, dear," she said, "When you are alone in your bed at night, and you hear gun shots in the distance, aren't you afraid?"

The poor dear! I was grateful for the opportunity to put her mind at ease. I explained I seldom if ever heard gun shots at night and I was not afraid. I knew danger was possible but I also knew we were not in the business of taking unnecessary risks.

As for my father, I think it is fair to say that his chest expanded just a little bit more when his daughter got her second medal: Canada's General Service Medal. My father and I were now equal in the medal department, with each of us having two of the shiny ornaments. It was very touching to know how proud he was of me. For my part, I was grateful he could recognize the value of what I was doing. His *pinko* daughter, as he had affectionately called me in my hippy phase in my twenties, was doing him proud. What an unexpected and pleasant surprise!

EPISODE VI

My 60s in Asia and Haiti

21. Three More Years on the Afghanistan Program

Y**ou may have noticed** I didn't talk about leaving the PRT in Kandahar in July 2009 probably because it was one of the least difficult places to leave. Yes, it was sad to come to the end of that experience, but it was clearly the most surreal of all my overseas adventures. By that I mean I had absolutely no wish to adopt that lifestyle for the rest of my days. Plus, I knew I was to continue to work on the Afghanistan program at headquarters in Ottawa and so it was not really saying goodbye. I was replaced by another adventurous bureaucrat with whom I would be in regular contact, as those are the symbiotic roles that colleagues in the field and at headquarters play.

Returning to Canada after a year on a military camp is not an easy thing to do. The good news was that as an indeterminate employee, at least I had a job to return to! I was essentially going to continue working on the same files, just from a different location. Furthermore, I was among colleagues who were relatively well equipped to understand the transition that I, the returnee, was experiencing. My hands-on experience was both recognized and appreciated as we continued to implement the education assistance program in Afghanistan.

The next year and a half of re-entry went by relatively smoothly. My boss asked me to hold the pen on the draft of an education strategy, which I did although without great joy. I am much more of a hands-on person but I was able to recognize the value of such a document. On the personal front, most of the time I was in la-la land with all the wonders of potable water from the tap and other plumbing that did not

179

require outdoor access. It was a pleasure to ditch the weight of the protective gear, to no longer have to wear a headscarf, and to end the day without being covered in layers of desert dust!

Alas however, as you no doubt know by now, I am not one to revel in luxury. Instead, within 18 months I was off on my next foray into Afghanistan. When I had initially applied to be posted there, I had wanted to go to the embassy in Kabul, but as you know that is not where I went. There were still opportunities at the embassy and so I headed there in December 2010. I would continue my work on the education files in Afghanistan, now from a third location.

In many ways, Kabul was everything I wanted and more. It was my first time as part of an embassy team. The ambassador was William (Bill) Crosbie, whom I already knew through his sister. Janet and I had gone to Trinity College, University of Toronto in our first year of university. We had rooms around the corner from each other at the residence of St. Hilda's across the street from the college. Janet and Bill are part of the Crosbie clan of St. John's, Newfoundland, and they are salt of the earth people. Janet and I have kept in touch all these years and through her I met Bill when I was living in Ottawa. I felt lucky to have this link with my first ambassador, especially as I was still new in diplomatic circles.

It was a large embassy. Many Canadians were posted there and we worked alongside Afghan colleagues. A Canadian Forces team was based there to provide close protection to the ambassador. As one of the Canadian civilians, I was kept safe by a team of British bodyguards, who escorted us when we traveled in armoured vehicles outside our compound. Again, I lived in a shipping container but this one was much larger, 40ft. x 10ft., and it had a full washroom as well as a miniature kitchen which was not really necessary as we ate our meals together in the cafeteria. Much of our food was imported from Dubai and skillfully prepared by a wonderful young cook from South Africa. But I neglected to mention that our containers were blast-proof. A friend referred to them affectionately as 'blast pods', an apt description! It is fair to say I felt safe in my container. Just to open the entry door of that armoured protection took my shoulders and body weight!

I could make many comparisons to my posting in Kandahar, on several levels. For now, I will stick with the physical ones. For starters, this was not a military camp. It was Canada's official sanctuary in Afghanistan. Although we had decent office space, we were not in individual offices but in a steno-like row of open-air cubicles. Noise pollution was a factor and there was virtually no privacy. We had good meeting spaces, although booking time in them was always a challenge.

We enjoyed a well-equipped gym and we needed it because there was no other way to get exercise. Although there was an above-ground pool of sorts, it paled in comparison to the Kandahar reservoir. Ironically, the neighbouring British Embassy had a wonderful in-ground pool but sadly I never managed to gain access to it. I could see it though from the top floor of our office and I would look at it longingly!

We had very little freedom of movement as it was not considered safe for us to venture forth on our own, nor would I have wanted to, to be honest. On a day off, we could sometimes book a vehicle and driver to take us to one of the military bases for their market days, shops and services. Under the right security conditions, we could occasionally go to a few approved restaurants and a wonderful boutique of Afghan crafts.

I have a handsome handmade carpet from there in my living room. It provides a fond memory of my posting in Kabul.

The other major difference between the postings in Kandahar and Kabul was that the embassy was far from being a dry zone. In fact, we had what was known as a Rec Centre, otherwise thought of as the Wreck Centre. It had a pool table and a bar of sorts and many social events were held there. Plus, there was no need for a no-fraternization policy in this adult environment. Let's just say that we worked out how to entertain ourselves when we were not working. I continued to play euchre and enjoyed the laughter and stress relief that game provided.

On the work front, I was super engaged. Canada was considered by the other donors as the lead country in the education sector. I was pleased I could bring a provincial perspective to the table, having spent a year working on education in Kandahar. We worked with a very cooperative Afghan Minister of Education – of course why would he not want to collaborate with the donors pouring millions of dollars into the Afghan education system? Canada was influential in setting up the Human Resource Development Board in the Ministry of Education and we co-chaired meetings with the Ministry there. This body was made up of the various departments of the Ministry and representatives of each donor country attended the regular meetings with them to advance the state of education in the country. By the time I left Afghanistan in May 2012, 16 months after arriving, the statistics indicated that school enrollment had increased to ten million or so, still with a third of that number girls. This marked a considerable accomplishment for the Afghan authorities in education, if those numbers were accurate.

Another achievement for the country during my time in Kabul was that Afghanistan became the 45th country to become a member of Education for All, a World Bank initiative out of Washington, DC. It was a lengthy and arduous application process for the Afghans to prove that their education system was up to world standards. The international community urged the Afghan Ministry of Education to lead on this as we accompanied them on their journey to be recognized for their progress despite the difficult circumstances.

Christmas away from home is something I have experienced in many places in the world. The memory of my first one in Kabul was quite touching. For some reason, I have always liked reading *How the Grinch Stole Christmas* so I offered to share it with my overseas Canadian family. Ambassador Crosbie suggested I give a reading for my colleagues in front of the fireplace at his residence. I remember it well, watching the softened eyes of some of the big burly men with whom I worked. It was a special moment.

During my second Christmas in Kabul, we were honoured by the visit of Canada's then-governor general, David Johnston, who came out to show our country's support of our personnel on the ground. His visit fell on Christmas Eve. That afternoon he met all of us in the top floor meeting room of the embassy. His comments were very moving as he recognized our efforts and our personal sacrifices to be there. I could not hold back the tears but I tried to be as discreet as possible. I even had to retreat to the nearby washroom for some tissue to wipe my leaking eyes!

Later that day, a reception for our esteemed visitor was held in the same room. Other Canadians working and living in Kabul were invited to attend. I remember having an interesting conversation with a police officer from Vancouver, when the governor general passed by to say good night. I was pleased to have the chance to tell him how much his remarks had touched me. I have a very clear memory of his response, "Well, I think that's what happens to us at this time of year!" Of course, it was hard to keep the tears from welling up yet again!

The circle of friends you make on a posting is a rich and diverse one. Living in such close quarters, we all got to know each other pretty well, as we ate, worked, exercised and played together. As in Kandahar, I had a similar range of work colleagues: most were from Foreign Affairs, as well as a handful from the Canadian Forces and Canadian police services. Fortunately, too, we were able to make friends with representatives from other embassies and agencies of the United Nations and the World Bank. Through our work we interacted with Afghans, both those who worked at our embassy and others who worked with the ministries where we were involved. We might also see them in a social setting such as an organized function at the embassy, but sadly we were not allowed to accept invitations to their homes. I was very fond of the three Afghan colleagues I worked with the most closely: Nazifa and Hikmat who were education advisers at our Program Support Unit, and Myriam, who was a project officer for education at the embassy.

People sometimes ask whether I was scared during my time in Kabul. I do have one strong memory of being in the bunker in the basement of our office building in April 2011. At the beginning of that month, insurgents had attacked a bunker in the UN compound in another town, Mazar-i-Sharif. Despite being sheltered, three international UN staff had been killed as well as four Nepali security staff. Just reading about this incident on Wikipedia in the writing of this section gave me the shivers.

But back to our bunker in Kabul – a complex attack was taking place in the area of our secure compound, which was the reason we were there under cover. As I sat there, I couldn't help but notice how inadequate the bolt on the door of our bunker looked. I was concerned that if we were under attack, it wouldn't hold. A bunker had not protected the UN staff earlier that month. Fortunately, it didn't come to that, but it was a long moment of fear and angst.

It was also fortunate that, a couple of months before that attack, I had been able to take a field trip to Herat, in the west of Afghanistan. We were four members of our education team plus a colleague from USAID. We went at the invitation of UNICEF who hosted us for the two or three days we were there. We were able to get out into the countryside to visit projects in community-based education. They were being implemented by civil society partners such as Save the Children and BRAC, a grassroots organization from Bangladesh. I have a strong visual memory of those outings. First of all, they were in barren rural settings and the classrooms were bare bones. The image I have still is of a lone female teacher in the front of a room with mud walls and a window with no glass or screen in it. There was one blackboard. I can't remember if there were desks. The children were young and wide-eyed. Just how much learning was going on, you had to wonder. It was still probably better than the children not being at school at all – at least I like to hope that was the case.

I wouldn't have had the courage to do that trip had it been scheduled after the attack in Mazar-i-Sharif. Nor would we have been given permission to go either, as approval for that sort of movement was the result of an extensive security assessment.

The 16 months I spent in Kabul were limited to that city, with the exception of the short trip to Herat. As in Kandahar, we were required to take R&Rs every eight weeks, and for those I was very grateful. For this posting they included a broad range:

- Algonquin Park in Ontario in August because where else in the world would you want to go at that time of year!
- An ayurvedic spa in the northeast of India, and an opportunity to visit the Taj Mahal.
- Trekking to see the gorillas in Rwanda with my Canadian friend Heather who helped me move my things to Ottawa. She was a volunteer teacher there at the time.
- A multi-sport trip to the Galapagos staying on three of the islands and not on a ship.
- Cruising on the Mekong River in Laos and exploring Cambodia.
- Cape Town in South Africa where I was able to meet up with my good friend Doug who had been such a great support in Ottawa before my posting to Kandahar.
- A beautiful idyllic resort on Koh Lanta in Thailand.

With the exception of Algonquin Park, I had been to none of the other places before and it was a delight to explore each of them. I can certainly say it resulted in my bucket list being significantly whittled down!

On finishing my 16-month tour in Afghanistan in May 2012, I was able to take several weeks off since I had accumulated so much overtime. My first stop was Nepal where a Canadian friend in Kabul had a base, and he was able to help arrange more adventures there, including teaching English for a week in the UNESCO World Heritage village of Bandipur. Next, I flew to Spain to teach English again but this time in an immersion setting with Spaniards whose tuition covered our expenses for up to a week in a resort area. I did this with two companies and then met up with another Canadian friend in Santiago de Compostela after her two weeks on the Camino. My final destination on that extended holiday was another inn-to-inn sea kayaking trip in Greece where we circumnavigated Santorini and its small neighbouring isle Thirasia. This surely was the life, these hardship postings!

I have two more stories related to this experience. They both exemplify my innate humanity, and let's face it, my humility. For context, allow me to explain what it is like to pack up your belongings following a Canadian government posting to a foreign land. I had been in Kabul for 16 months. My lodgings had been furnished and I was not cooking for myself so that cut down on the volume of possessions. However, it still takes a fair bit of thought and organizing to gather them all together and make up a detailed inventory, along with the replacement cost value. My shipment was picked up in early April 2012. After that I still had one R&R, and then on leaving Kabul at the end of April, I would be travelling to three countries over an 11-week period.

I became aware of the first mishap, yes, these were trying experiences to say the least, in the plane on the way from Kabul to Nepal. I was happily engaged in conversation with the man sitting next to me on the plane, when all of a sudden, I realized I had left something very important in the top drawer of my dresser in the blast pod container that had been home for 16 months. It was a small mesh bag containing my supply of underwear for the next 11 weeks!

Oh my, I couldn't believe it and I couldn't keep this huge mistake to myself. But who was I to tell except for the man sitting next to me? He listened politely but no doubt could not begin to relate to my dilemma. First of all, most men do not wear brassieres, so that would not have mattered one iota to him. Secondly, most men can easily purchase underpants wherever they are. For me in Nepal this was another matter entirely. I will spare you the precise details of my body measurements but let me just say I am larger than your average Nepali woman, not to mention that Nepal just might not be on the distribution list for such brand names as Wonderbra, my preferred choice.

Once I had settled at my accommodation in Kathmandu, I made a call to a Nepali man whose name I had been given, perhaps by my Canadian friend Peter in Kabul but I'm not sure. He was warm and kind, saying he and his wife would like to meet me, and in fact they invited me to their home for a meal. Near the end of the first conversation, he asked if there was anything I needed. Well, yes, as a matter of fact, there was. I proceeded to ask him where in Kathmandu I could buy panties and bras! Off I went the next day in search of said articles.

Fortunately, Lycra is stretchy and I managed to get some articles that would do, but just barely, so to speak! To end this little story, I prevailed on my good Canadian friend, Barb Shaw, to bring me a couple of Wonderbra's for when we were to meet up in Spain, but that was still a good three weeks away. End of that story!

The second mishap took place during what were to be my last 12 hours in Spain before leaving for Greece. Within that 12-hour period, I was robbed twice in two

Spanish cities, first Madrid and then Barcelona! After that second hit, I wanted to lie down on the floor of the Barcelona train station and throw a temper tantrum. Seriously, I was done. It was all too much. Here's what happened.

On my last evening in Madrid, I had treated myself to a manicure. I mention this because it played a role in my remembering I had carefully closed the U-shaped zipper on my purse which I could wear as a backpack. First mistake, you might be thinking. Yes, I had my purse on my back.

It was about 8:00 p.m. on a bright summer evening. I was in a small shop in a respectable part of the capital city. It was crowded and I was being pushed around a bit. I remember turning around and looking directly at the woman who appeared to be pushing me. Afterwards, I realized I had probably looked right at the culprit who had managed to open that U-shaped zipper and extract my wallet.

I was not aware of what had happened until I went to leave the shop and for some reason, I just checked the weight of my bag. Sure enough, I could tell it was lighter. I panicked and went back into the shop but to no avail. I returned to the shop where I had had the manicure just in case my wallet had been left there. It had not.

I was in a bit of a pickle. I had a ticket for a night train to Barcelona, where the next morning I was to catch a flight to Greece. How was I going to make that happen? I returned to the hotel where I had left my luggage. Fortunately, I speak Spanish and I was able to ask the hotel staff for some help in calling Visa about my stolen credit card but it was just the tip of the iceberg. My diplomatic passport had been in the stolen wallet but fortunately I still had my personal passport with me. What I did not have was any cash nor did I have any way of getting more cash.

Many surprising things happened in this story and here is the first one. The hotel manager, who had overheard my story, gave me 100 Euro out of his pocket! I was astonished and at the same time extremely grateful, having not a cent to my name at that point. First lesson learned here: don't keep all your money in one place!

I dragged my sorry butt to the Madrid train station, anxious about what fate I might meet on my eight-hour night journey to Barcelona. I slept sporadically with my few remaining valuables clutched to my chest. We, the valuables and I, made it through the night but then I made my second mistake. I had a money pouch I could wear around my neck but I decided I didn't need it. Why, you might well ask, would I make such a foolish decision? Hello! Am I not some intrepid traveler who knows better? Apparently not.

Into the Barcelona train station I went with my copious amount of luggage. I had a bag on my back, two suitcases on wheels, plus my purse, which was not on my back this time. I had this volume of luggage because by now it had been eight weeks since my shipment had been picked up in Kabul. I should have sent more with the movers so I could have traveled lightly on my circuitous route back to Canada.

I went to the information booth to ask about buying a train ticket to get to the airport. The attendant took me over to a vending machine and explained the procedure. I put my luggage down around me. My purse I looped over the extended draw handle of one of my suitcases which was at my side. I then tried to insert a 20 Euro bill into the machine. It kept rejecting the bill. I tried four times. And then, you guessed it, I looked down and my whole purse was gone! In less than a minute, really. I was gobsmacked. Still as I write this, I have a visceral reaction to this last coup. I called out for help but the culprits were

190

extremely efficient and fast. No one was in sight and I was hardly in a position to go chasing after anyone anyway. Perhaps you can understand why that tantrum I mentioned earlier was imminent. On the other hand, I wanted to curl up in a ball on the floor and just give up. Of course, I didn't. That is not the stuff I'm made of.

This time, I was in even worse shape than after the incident in Madrid. I really, really dragged myself out of the station. I could not continue to Greece. Now my personal passport was also gone. Fortunately, I had learned at least a little bit from the first hit, and I had kept about 30 Euro in a pocket. I still had my little flip cell phone, which came in handy. Other than that, I had lost my camera and my Samsung tablet, along with personal items such as a comb and lipstick. What's a gal to do without those last two items?

To add insult to injury (I now really know what that means), as I was shlepping all my gear down the street to the police station, I walked past a building which was being painted. I ended up being spattered with paint – don't ask me how. It certainly added to my bag-lady appearance. My sorry butt now qualified as a very sorry ass, which was truly tested as it was dragged a seemingly endless distance to report these egregious events.

At the police station, they were as helpful as they could be under the circumstances. Again, I was so grateful I could communicate in their language, although my Spanish is that of Latin America, but they were able to follow me. I had a photocopy of my documents which helped a bit.

Here is where the silver lining starts shining through, again. It was a very odd chain of events. Someone in Madrid had found my stolen wallet. Apparently, the custom is to take the cash (in this case about 300 Euro), and then dump the wallet. An individual had looked at my diplomatic passport and called the emergency number in it. Now the Department of Foreign Affairs in Ottawa was aware of my dilemma – although I am not sure that helped much. It was a Saturday morning and there was no one at the Canadian consulate in Barcelona who was interested in helping out a fellow colleague. I must say that surprised me. How naïve am I? I didn't get a new passport until the following Tuesday.

I had been able to communicate with the travel company, Northwest Passage, which was running the kayak trip in Greece. It was to have started on the Sunday, the day after the second hit but of course I wasn't able to arrive in time. Since I had done four other trips with this company, I knew the CEO, Rick Sweitzer, who was leading the trip. Only two other people had signed up – a couple from New Zealand. Rick had dinner with them on the Saturday evening and then oddly enough, they suddenly had to return home on the Sunday morning due to the death of a close friend.

So, there was Rick with no guests for the tour. Being the intrepid fellow he is, he used the additional three days to check out another Greek island for a future tour. I am happy to report he met me at the airport on Tuesday afternoon, and we then did the seven-day tour in five fast days. After the second day I was exhausted from all the paddling and Rick wisely decided to switch to a double kayak. I swallowed my pride and gratefully accepted his strong paddling in the stern. The trip was fabulous, as always. It even included my new Visa card being delivered at lunch at one of our coastal restaurants along the way! Talk about serendipity! Actually, I guess it was really more than that. It was simply good planning on Rick's part.

There is more to the story of the found wallet. The person also noticed a slip of paper in my wallet with a

Spanish phone number on it. He called the number and found he was speaking to one of the Spaniards who had been in the English program where I had been teaching. As I said, there are some bizarre twists of fate in this story. The Spanish student in turn got in touch with another Canadian woman who had been teaching there. She was still in Madrid but on her way to Barcelona – of course! She arranged to meet the person who had my wallet at the hotel where I had stayed. She was not able to repay the hotel manager but I made that arrangement later with my good friend from Ottawa, Doug, who had also come to Spain, on my suggestion, to teach English.

So I got my wallet back in Barcelona although by then the credit card had been cancelled. How did I manage without any money until she arrived? I could not even have money wired to me as I had no identification! I walked around town looking for a reasonable hotel which would accept payment from my dear brother Liam's credit card! What a fiasco! Two other people came to my rescue. They were guests at the hotel where I was staying. They had overheard me telling my story to the hotel clerk and offered me 20 Euro so I could have dinner that evening. What kindness on their part! When my Canadian friend arrived safely in Barcelona with the contents of my wallet, I was finally able to use my debit card to get some much-needed cash.

The last time I had been robbed was 28 years previously in La Paz, Bolivia, where I had lost only my camera. That was an amateur show compared to what I had experienced in Spain. I will say it was really humbling to find out what it feels like to be close to destitute when you are alone, and in another country, far away from your support network. My brother rallied as did the two people I'd met teaching English but many of the others who had helped me out had been complete strangers. I'm grateful to have survived the trauma. Of course, it could have been a lot worse. I'm very glad it was not.

22. The Sunny Caribbean

While **working in Kabul** in Afghanistan, I remember thinking I would not apply for another posting. After 16 months away it was time to go back to reality in Canada. However, that meant returning home in the summer of 2012 to the continuing Conservative government of Stephen Harper, who appeared to dislike Canada's public service and its civil servants. You have to admit it is pretty bad when the political environment in Canada is enough to drive you away to live in other countries where governance is decidedly worse. But that is what happened.

I acknowledge it was not the sole reason I changed my mind early in 2012 about possibly going on another adventure. Truth be told, when the posting list came out from headquarters in Ottawa, I was very excited to see there was a vacancy in Barbados! This appealed hugely and I thought my family and friends would surely come to visit me there! Of course, I applied, with visions of palm trees, sandy beaches and sunshine very much front of mind.

The opposite of a posting in Afghanistan in terms of hardship, I recognized there would be stiff competition for Barbados. So, wisely, I also applied for a posting in Haiti which would be a bit of a stretch as it would be in French, which I spoke, but I had never been on a program that was primarily conducted in French. An advantage of both postings was that they were in the same time zone as Ottawa, and therefore only a two- or three-hour time difference from my family in Western Canada. That would be one heck of an improvement over the time difference of 11 or 12 and a half hours in Afghanistan.

Well, as my mother used to tell me, life is not always fair, and sure enough, I didn't even get an interview for the position in Barbados. The Haiti program, however, was keen on my candidacy. I think it may well have been because one of the decision makers there was probably routing for me. Roger Roome and I had first met in the early 1990s when I was working with World University Service of Canada and he was with CIDA. The details are no longer very clear but we overlapped at that time for the briefing of students from the Caribbean coming to Canada to study. Over ten years later in 2003, work brought us together again, and Roger still had my business card! Fast forward another nine years and up he pops again, this time at our embassy in Haiti, playing a role in my immediate future.

The good news is that my posting in Haiti was a pretty good fit. It even included palm trees, sandy beaches and sunshine – just what I had been dreaming about. After my extended time off, I returned to Ottawa in the summer of 2012. For a couple of weeks I worked at CIDA headquarters on the Haiti desk, and then began my posting in Haiti in mid-August. It was two and a half years since the devastating earthquake had hit Haiti and killed over 200,000 people and there were still many signs of damage. A natural disaster of that magnitude would cause a major setback for any developed country but for the poorest country in the Western Hemisphere, it created a horrendous challenge.

The powers that be appeared to be smiling upon me again. Perhaps it had something to do with having lived in a conflict zone. The first and biggest blessing that came my way was the housing assigned to me. I had expected to live in another 'blast pod', i.e., an armoured container like the one in Kabul, although the model in Haiti had three small rooms, making it square instead of rectangular.

Apparently, the head of aid, who was participating in this decision and who did not know me personally, thought it was unfair to ask me to live in another container after doing so for 28 months in Afghanistan. Instead, I was assigned a splendid villa overlooking the city. It was handsomely furnished which was a good thing because there were three bedrooms, four and a half bathrooms (seriously!), a family room, a kitchen that reminded me of ones you would find in Canada, a dining room with a table that seated ten, a bowling alley-like veranda, a garage, a garden, and – are you ready? – a swimming pool! Oh my, I had arrived in heaven. There were palm trees too and soon enough I strung a hammock between two of them to reap the benefits of the palm trees and sunshine I had dreamed of.

To manage my new-to-me estate, the embassy paid 75% of the salary for a gardener, Félix, who also maintained the pool. It was up to me to engage a housekeeper, although it was my choice whether I did so or not. I was happy to provide employment for Paulène, who was a gem, and who had previously worked for my colleague Roger during his posting there. As well, the Embassy paid for four armed guards, who took 12-hour shifts to protect me and the property 24/7.

It is important to mention I did pay rent for these luxurious quarters, whereas the blast pod would have been free. I was happy to oblige and the amount was in line with what I would have been paying in Ottawa for a two-bedroom apartment with nowhere near the panache of my new digs. In defence of the embassy providing me such comfort, I can explain that it was very hard to find anything between an unsuitable shack and what I got, a villa. There was not a lot of room for the middle class in Haiti.

I will add that my residence was the closest to the embassy which made a huge difference in commuting time as rush hour traffic in the capital city of Port-au-Prince was a major issue. I could get to work in as little as 15 minutes, while it took many of my colleagues at least three times as long. It meant though that I didn't have any colleagues as neighbours, except those down in the blast-proof containers at the embassy.

It is also relevant to mention that I was not allowed to go to work any other way than by car, as it was not considered safe to walk or ride a bike. Neither were we allowed to use the 'tap-taps', the local public transport so-named because when you wanted to get off, you tap-tapped the side of the vehicle. Other factors were the hills and the fact it was too warm and dusty to be on the roads in anything but an air-conditioned vehicle. The tap-taps had natural air-conditioning as they were open to the elements. For the most part I took advantage of the embassy cars and drivers which provided a shuttle service to and from the office at a minimum monthly charge. This was a great way to go since I didn't have to deal with the traffic and it allowed me time to get to know our Haitian drivers. It also helped regulate my hours at the office and that I really appreciated, especially after the very long hours I had worked in Afghanistan.

We started early at the office (7:00 a.m.) to have some daylight between the end of the workday at 3:30 p.m. and sundown around 6:30 p.m. as I recall. These hours were contrary to my norm, which was more like nine to five. Nevertheless, I managed to get into the tropical rhythm and enjoyed swimming lengths in the embassy pool after hours, and still managed to catch the shuttle home. This was a wonderful way to end the workday. Although I had a pool at home, it was not big enough to do laps.

Some days the regular hours were not possible. We left the office to go on field trips to visit our projects which provided welcome forays into the countryside, checking in with reality outside the capital city. We were always well received, of course, because we were the donors but I like to think there was some genuine interest in meeting us *blancs* (the French word for white folk).

Another comparison with my last posting was my relative freedom of movement in Haiti. What most Canadians don't know is that the Government of Canada will pay for a large shipment to the country where you are posted. This may include shipping a vehicle, which is what I did because I really wanted to be able to move around after so much time not having that liberty. So, on occasion, I did drive myself to the office if the shuttle schedule was not going to work for me that day.

I was not allowed to drive everywhere as there were some insecure zones but most of the places I wanted to go were considered safe. For the most part it included the beaches to the north of the city, although it was a long drive. It was possible to make it a day trip but ideally, I would go with friends for a weekend getaway whenever possible. Going in the other direction, to the southwest of the city, I had to have an armed guard in my vehicle until we got through the rough part of town. Then the following escort vehicle would take the guard back to the city and I would be on my way. On the return a rendezvous on the outskirts of town was required before driving through the dodgy district to the safety of my home. This might not have been everyone's cup of tea but it was still pretty easy after the restrictions on movement in Afghanistan.

I settled in quite nicely despite the fact there was a hurricane within a week of my arrival in Port-au-Prince. It tempts me to say that I took the city by storm! The hurricane proved to be a mild one but it was followed a few months later by Hurricane Sandy which took a huge toll all the way up the east coast of the US to New York City. Our homes were clearly secure in such storms but the same cannot be said for the many Haitians who lived in tents. The poverty was quite overwhelming. I often describe life for many Haitians as full-time camping and we are not talking some idyllic, well-serviced provincial campground. *Au contraire.* Even a nighttime foray to a latrine was hazardous for a woman as she might be sexually assaulted en route.

Life in Haiti is not for the faint-hearted. The resilience of the Haitian people, though, defies description. It may boil down to the simple fact there is no choice. Most of the neighbouring countries require visas for Haitians to visit them, and they are very hard to come by. Then there is the inflation of the gourd, the local currency. When I arrived in 2012, it cost about 42 gourds to buy a US dollar. By the time I left three years later a dollar cost about 64 gourds, which continue to lose value.

The economic troubles in Venezuela have affected Haiti, since the former used to subsidize the cost of fuel for the latter. This is no longer the case and the severe unrest in Haiti early in 2019 was related to this harsh reality for Haitians. Even the basics such as water and sanitation, which we take for granted, are not available to many Haitians. In 2014, then-president Michel Martelly, who had formerly been a pop singer in America, decided to spruce up one of the poorer neighbourhoods called Jalousie by painting those hillside homes in Port-au-Prince in bright, cheerful colours. It may have looked picturesque but it fell far short of providing the basic necessities of potable water and a sewer system. It is sobering to think this poverty exists in a country less than two hours' flight from Miami.

I am often asked why the Dominican Republic, the country on the leeward side of the same island, known as Hispaniola, has done so much better than Haiti, for example in tourism. I have yet to find an adequate answer. Sometimes I point out the simple difference in geography, the fact that Haiti is on the windward side of the island and bears the brunt of weather systems. Then, I might mention the different colonizers, the French versus the Spanish, but we cannot forget that Haiti became the first black republic in 1804 and so has ruled itself for more than two centuries, unfortunately in a very harsh way. Some veteran expatriates in Haiti will look to the habit of relying on hand-outs – maybe this is part of the malaise.

It is important to note that the Dominican Republic is not without its trials. Many Haitians work there or at least they used to before the Dominican Republic ruled that all Haitians born there since 1929 had to leave the country. That happened in 2014, and it was not pretty. I am not sure where that situation stands today. Suffice it to say, many Haitians avoid going to the Dominican Republic if they can, but those who need work do not have a choice, considering the high unemployment rate in Haiti.

I felt fortunate I had the opportunity to explore Haiti. I have always preferred to look around where I am instead of going too far afield – what an ironic declaration from the perpetual traveler that I am! What I am trying to say is that I did not choose to venture to the other side of Hispaniola until I had had a good look around my immediate environs. Besides, one of my friends was the indomitable Jacqualine Labrom, a British expatriate who runs a busy travel agency, Voyages Lumière, in Port-au-Prince. She organized incredible adventures and I benefited from many of them. Two stand out in my memory, both destinations beautiful in their own way.

The first involved a day-long boat ride to Mole St. Nicolas where Christopher Columbus is said to have landed in the northwest of Haiti. We knew it would be a long journey but we had no idea how long. We arrived at the boat launch early in the day to get started before the heat of day. Well, it was like the military: hurry up and wait! We were not sure what the delays were: mechanical possibly, or maybe crew? We eventually learned it may have been mechanical as the 20ft. cabin cruiser could not reach a reasonable speed and we had a long way to go. What lay ahead was far worse. The sea got rough and the engine started to blow out clouds of soot! That made it unpleasant to be out in the open air but unfortunately those inside the cabin were suffering from motion sickness so the air quality there was also an assault on the senses.

By the time we arrived at our destination, dusk was upon us. We were both filthy and hungry but we had arrived at a tropical paradise. Well, let us say that nature fit the bill – the human installations a little less so. Serving food to our group of ten took a long time and when we got to our lodgings, we discovered a few things were lacking: toilet paper, soap, bottled water and the power was off. It wasn't as if we could go to the local corner store as we were outside of a small village. We were disappointed but we were safe, our bellies were full, and we were off the water before nightfall. Despite the rough first day, we loved the rest of our three-day visit where few other tourists venture.

We had to return by boat but, thankfully, it was a different vessel. Again, the sea was rough making the return journey quite hard on the old bodies! But we made it, with vivid memories of a long weekend well spent!

The other trip was equally adventurous. We took a small boat over to Île de la Tortue from the northwest town of Port-de-Paix where we had flown from Port-au-Prince. On the first full day we traveled by boat to the western tip of the island and one of the ten most beautiful beaches in the Caribbean, according to Condé Nast Traveler in 1996. It had the shining white sand and turquoise waters, and it was deserted except for a few locals who had come to check out the latest visitors. There were no amenities and little shade. Although it was picturesque, I wouldn't have ranked it in the top ten.

The island was renowned as a pirate hangout. We got an inkling of this infamy in what might have been a drug lord's villa. We were such a big group that two of us had to go to this overflow location. It was a large, cavernous white-washed structure stuck in the middle of nowhere. The owners were not there nor do I remember meeting them. There were no other guests. The furnishings were sparse although we each had a room with a bed and an en suite bathroom. But the towels for example still had their sales tags on them. I think we stayed only two or three nights, which was fine. It was an unusual experience.

The other places I loved to visit were resorts near Cap-Haitien in the north, Labadie in particular, as well as those just a couple of hours drive north of Port-au-Prince, near Montrouis. To the south of the capital city was Jacmel, Île à Vache, Port Salut and to the west, Petit-Goâve. I even got to Jérémie in the far southwest where I traveled for work. One day there we drove over very rough roads for about eight hours to visit projects implemented by Care Canada. I kept hoping there would be a public toilet of some kind to relieve my bursting bladder but alas there was not. I thought that a visit to a school would be the answer. When it was not, I finally had to ask where I might take care of business.

My needs were understandable but it was still awkward. In the end, the solution was in someone's two-room home. The gracious host offered me the equivalent of a bedpan and provided the relative privacy of her second room. Afterwards, she gave me a basin, water and soap so I could wash my hands. It was a first-hand look at another harsh reality.

Having more or less set the scene of this new posting, I want to write a little about my work in Haiti. I will say it was probably the most difficult work I have ever done. First of all, as I mentioned earlier, everything was in French, and I was determined to make that work. That meant I spoke only French with all my colleagues, Canadian and Haitian alike.

After about three months of this effort, I was pretty exhausted and I had a little chat with myself. It went something like this, "Wait a minute here. I am a federal public servant for a country that has two official languages. I am an Anglophone and as such, I have the right to speak my mother tongue!" Once in a while, with my Canadian colleagues, I would do just that. To my surprise, almost all of them spoke very good English. The surprise was not about their ability in this regard, but rather the fact they had not reverted to English when I was speaking to them in French. For those who have not had this experience in Ottawa or Montreal, for example, this is what usually happens to Anglophones who try to practice their French. In fact, from my perspective, I had come out the winner because my francophone colleagues had given me ample opportunity to improve my French! You could say it was a win-win scenario, for which I was grateful.

I have said the work in Haiti was not easy, one reason being that it was in my second language. That was a personal reason. The others are related to the sectors in which I was working. Public servants are often generalists, so it is not uncommon to be asked to work in many different sectors. This was the case in Haiti where I took on the files in governance and humanitarian assistance. The latter is what most people think of when you work in development.

It was the first time I had been assigned to cover what you may know as aid. This is a concrete dossier in that it involves the way Canada responds to the immediate needs of a developing country in the case of a natural disaster. But you might think that, in between disasters, the workload would drop off. This is not so, because it is a good time to build the capacity of the country's institutions to provide for the well-being of its population. The UN agency leading this work on the part of the donors is the Office for the Coordination of Humanitarian Affairs (OCHA). Weekly meetings were held for representatives from all the stakeholders in order to share information. It was an excellent way to become immersed in my new setting by meeting the participants and learning what each of their organizations was doing in post-earthquake Haiti. I was pleased to follow the humanitarian assistance files for two years before passing them on to another colleague.

My other files, or projects, were related to governance, which meant trying to strengthen the capacity of the state's public institutions to serve the people. Your eyes may well glaze over at this task especially in the poorest country in the Western

Hemisphere. It is without a doubt a rather abstract sector and more difficult to identify progress or measure results. It was quite the opposite of the concrete sector of education which I had worked on in Afghanistan. However, I can mention some of the projects I monitored to bring some clarity to this abstract sector.

Canada had committed a considerable budget to support the Haitian government in building a national police academy. It meant not just the physical structure but also the soft side of designing programming and developing curriculum. Canada's implementing partner for this initiative was a private sector firm in Montreal and the project was rolled out in collaboration with Quebec colleges that trained senior ranks of the police. Now this was pretty concrete but it was a constant challenge, partly to ensure the Canadian institutions were functioning in such a way as to accompany the Haitians in this initiative. The objective was not to replace the Haitians responsible for the academy. They would need to operate on their own at the end of the project. To give you an idea of how difficult that was, it may help to know that the whole Haitian police service had an annual operating budget of only $15,000 US. I think that was separate from the budget line for staffing but nevertheless, it was grossly insufficient for items such as vehicles, fuel, office space, equipment and all the other items required to ensure the security of nearly ten million inhabitants.

On the fringes of this project, Canada stepped forward to help Haiti restore its fire-fighting department. For over a year we tried to get all the elements of this initiative in place but when my posting ended in 2015, we were still not ready to launch the project. I don't know if it was ever successful although I think it was not, despite the desperate need for infrastructure to provide a fire-fighting service to Haitians.

More traditional governance projects involved strengthening public administration by linking Quebec experts with Haitian counterparts. Canada's École nationale de l'administration publique (ÉNAP) took the lead on this project, which was in the very capable hands of a Haitian Canadian woman, Magalie Cadet Rodrigue, who worked tirelessly in Port-au-Prince to facilitate these connections. Progress was made by various individuals but the strengthening of the Haitian government ministries involved was difficult to measure.

A similar project provided technical assistance to government officials with the aim of building up the capacity of their public institutions. This was perhaps even more challenging for a myriad of reasons that do not merit description here. Suffice it to say that many individuals benefitted from this project but whether it contributed to strengthening public institutions was uncertain.

A cross-cutting theme of this governance work was promoting equality between women and men. Haiti has a Department of Women's Affairs and the international donors, including Canada, accompanied the Haitian officials as they finalized their long-awaited policy on gender equality. This had been in the works for several years and so it was important when it was accepted by the senior Haitian government authorities. The policy was complemented by a gender equality action plan to set the principles of the policy in motion. This initiative took place near the end of my time in Haiti in 2015 so I am not sure whether or not it was implemented, especially because a new government was subsequently elected.

The other governance project I followed was one designed to build the capacity of Haiti's public institutions involved in holding democratic elections. Canada's partner was the National Democratic Institute based in Washington, DC. Its country representative in Haiti was Canadian Jane Hurtig, who gave her all to get results. Naturally I was enthusiastic about this project, given my many years working in election administration in the Balkans. It was easier to see results on this project in Haiti since relatively peaceful elections were conducted in August 2015. But that was only one measure of success; five years later, the country is in a relative mess politically despite our best efforts to the contrary.

I learned a lot from my work but one hot topic managed to evade me and that was corruption. I am often asked what I saw in that regard. In fact, with one minor exception, I saw nothing I could put my finger on. I can tell you the role of a field officer such as myself is to be the eyes and ears on the ground. My job was gathering local intelligence to share with colleagues in headquarters. I had to ensure the investment of Canadian tax dollars was going where it was meant to go and I can assure you it was. Reporting on project progress, both in a narrative and financial format, is frequent and demanding. Further disbursements are not provided until previous ones are reported on and accounted for.

Inevitably, I end up going back to the personal. This is, after all, my life story! There is still more to tell you about my experiences in Haiti.

A blend of the personal and professional took place part way through my three-year stay in Haiti. As you know, some Canadian government procedures can take rather a long time and it was certainly the case here. While in Haiti, I had the honour of being given Canada's Operational Service Medal for the 16 months I had spent working at our embassy in Kabul. Another colleague and I received this award in a ceremony hosted by our embassy in Haiti. This moment brought the total number of my medals to three. My father was extremely proud even if it meant his daughter now had one more medal than he had!

You may remember the posting in Barbados had initially caught my eye because I thought family and friends would surely come to visit me there. Well, surprisingly enough, in Haiti I had the pleasure of visits from nine hardy souls whose curiosity drove them to venture to the poorest country in the Western Hemisphere. I loved showing them around and they lapped up the variety of sights and experiences. In Petionville, the upmarket neighbourhood of Port-au-Prince, we dined out and went to a small, crowded *boîte de nuit* with live music (at least one saxophone if not two), and the sultry kompa, the national dance I have heard called the Haitian tango. We drove to beaches and stayed in cozy cottage-like resorts. We walked up in the hills above the city, visiting expatriates I had got to know, enjoying the cooler mountain air and feasting our eyes on the unexpected pine trees and endless vistas. All through our wanderings we soaked up the bright sunlight and vibrant colours of Haiti.

Once I was driving with guests through a Saturday morning roadside market, which by the way, was the main 'highway'. As we had slowed to a crawl, I asked if anyone would like me to play a CD. The response was, "Oh, no thank you. I am already very over-stimulated." On another occasion, in a similar setting, one of my guests said something along these lines, "It's all so interesting, but it's just not pretty!" That summed it up quite well but my guests learned that there was beauty in Haiti despite the overwhelming poverty.

Having just mentioned Barbados, that's another story. Before the end of my first year in Haiti, I decided to visit a Canadian friend, Jean McCardle, who had worked with me in Afghanistan. Jean was then posted to our high commission in Bridgetown. I went for five days, an extended weekend. While Jean was working, I relaxed by the pool at the compound where she lived. When she was free, we went touring around the island to see the sights. Jean was kind enough to invite friends over for dinner so I could meet some of her expatriate friends. It's hard to explain, but that visit helped me realize I would have been bored to tears in Barbados. It was simply too conservative for me. Those attracted to live and work there were less likely to be risk-takers, the latter being my kind of peeps. Jean fit into the latter category! After all, we had become friends working together in both Kandahar and Kabul.

Haiti, on the other hand, was the complete opposite. One particularly good mechanism to meet a broad range of those attracted to live and work in Haiti was a small library that lent English books. The Library Club of Haiti was located in the Petionville Club which had tennis courts and a good-sized pool. It was expensive to join that club but the library was a mere $35 US per year. The library was open every Friday after work, and although we went to borrow books, it was almost secondary to the socializing. Every other Friday we had a *ti-wine, ti* from the French word *petit* (small). Essentially it was a wine and cheese, provided by the members, whose turn came up to bring either the wine or the hors-d'oeuvres only once a year. We were a diverse cast of characters and I made good friends there. Some of the expats had been in Haiti for as long as 35 years, in some cases having come for just a few months but finding no reason to leave, or perhaps deciding to marry their Haitian teacher of Créole! They were businesspeople, missionaries, teachers, humanitarian workers, diplomats, you name it. I thrived from the stimulation of it all.

On Monday evenings, I played kitchen bridge at the home of the president of the library, Canadian Tom Adamson and his lovely Haitian wife, Monica. We often had two tables and here too we were characters, including two Haitian sisters, easily in their eighties. One was a very strong bridge player, the other not so much. It was not always harmonious but it was never dull!

In terms of making friends with Haitians, that was less straightforward. In my earlier days working overseas with non-governmental organizations, I enjoyed getting to know the locals. This was not as easy, I was soon to discover, when you are attached to a Canadian Embassy, as I was in both Haiti and Afghanistan. The irony is that in Afghanistan there were gestures on the part of my Afghan colleagues to socialize outside of work but due to the tight security measures, it was not possible. In Haiti, where security was much less of an issue and where I had my own vehicle, I was rarely invited to spend time with my local colleagues outside the office. I could understand this. In the first place, why would locals want to invest in making friends with people who are going to leave the country after their one-, two- or three-year assignment? There was also the chicken and egg scenario. Was I not available to be friends with the locals because I was always with the ex-pats, or was I always with the expats because there were no locals to hang out with?

Nevertheless, I did get to know some of the Haitians who worked at my house. I have already mentioned my housekeeper, Paulène, who came three times a week. She was a godsend in many ways. I have never lived in such a clean house and as I said, it was a big place to keep clean. Although it was usually just me at home, dust was a major factor. It was a good idea to keep bugs at bay. Small ants could be troublesome, so I always had to be sure to seal food containers. I was not always successful with my morning cereal as I discovered one day, fortunately before I started to eat, that the contents of the bowl were moving! They were some kind of very small worms that thought they had gone to heaven with the feast provided and sure enough, that is exactly where they went!

Paulène went to the local fruit and vegetable markets for me. That was a blessing, since my presence as a *blanc* (white) at a local market would have resulted in excessive attention not to mention higher prices. Then Paulène would peel and chop the fruit for the fridge, and often fry up thin plantain chips, which I loved. I translated recipes to French for her so I could enjoy other favorites such as spiced okra, a veggie readily available in the tropics. Paulène even made granola for me!

I had fewer interactions with Félix, the gardener, so I did not get to know him well. Of the four guards, one was particularly warm and friendly. As we kept in touch after I left, I managed to have a visit with Nickenson a year after I had returned to Canada. I went back to Haiti on a work mission and took some personal time at the end. I invited him, his wife, mother and two small boys to the hotel pool for a visit. It was fun to reconnect in such a different venue from the garage of my villa!

As outsiders, we sometimes ended up having intimate conversations that might be uncomfortable for locals to have with people they know. For example, in a chat with one guard about his wife being pregnant with their fourth child, I told him about IUDs and about a hospital where his wife could be treated at a very reasonable cost. The hospital is two hours out of

Port-au-Prince in Mirebalais, where an NGO known as Partners in Health has created a modern health facility with a wide range of services. I knew about this through my good friend Elizabeth Campa, a Cuban–American dedicated to this organization.

As for other pastimes, a special one for me in Haiti was a monthly spa day, usually held at my house but sometimes at the equally lovely villa of my colleague Nathalie. About four to eight women would gather on a Saturday for massage, manicures and pedicures provided by Haitian practitioners. Everybody brought a healthy dish to share throughout the day and we lounged around the pool in between massages and during the mani/pedis. Those days bring back fond memories and funny ones too. Once we had planned our gathering to include a birthday celebration. We came together around the table in the dining room to sing Happy Birthday. The candles were blown out and the cake cut, only to discover the store-bought cake was laced with mould! Having lived in Haiti for a while and being accustomed to such things, we all burst out laughing at this unintended dose of penicillin unwittingly provided for our celebration!

I can't resist mentioning a couple of big parties I hosted in my grand digs. First, though, I will tell you I decided to take up a hobby I had planned to start in retirement – to learn to play the saxophone. It came about when a fellow Canadian introduced me to a Haitian saxophone player. Why delay? I asked myself. Here was a perfect opportunity: a teacher and a place to practice where I wouldn't bother anyone. Although it was an interesting exercise, it was not very successful. It turned out I was not enamoured with the approach to adult education of my local teacher, who was my vintage. Plus, I wanted more immediate results, even though I was not inclined to put in enough time to

213

practice. I did learn to play Happy Birthday and a couple of Christmas carols but in the end, we quarreled, and I have not picked up the saxophone since.

But back to the parties. The first one was called 'Sax in the Garden', and the second was 'More Sax in the Garden'. My music teacher played at them both and they were great fun! We set up a keyboard in the bowling alley veranda which looked out onto the garden and the pool. Haitian and expat alike enjoyed the seductive rhythms and the late afternoon breezes. The oldest guest was 90, the father of my colleague Nathalie. He had traveled from Montreal to visit his daughter who was on her ninth posting! From Haiti she cross-posted to Jamaica and I indulged in a visit there over Christmas one year.

A less pleasant memento from Haiti was breaking my right (dominant) elbow in September 2014. I was on my way to work one Friday morning but as usual I was a bit rushed. I had my arms full of things for the day, including two lamps I had to return to the embassy. In my haste I hadn't bothered to wrap up the cords and sure enough, I tripped on one of them and fell down nine ceramic stairs. I ended up at the bottom, sitting like a rag doll. Luckily, I was still conscious but I could tell there was something wrong with my arm. I realized in retrospect much later the accident could have been so much worse. I shudder to think.

Nevertheless, it was a very bad break which required surgery in Haiti. The surgeon was educated at McGill University in Montreal, where there is a large Haitian population. I think the surgery itself was what was needed but the post-operative care was perhaps not the best. I did physiotherapy four times a week for five months, both at the surgeon's office and with a private physiotherapist educated in the Dominican Republic. Finally, in March 2015 I saw a surgeon in Ottawa and he recommended arthroscopic surgery which I had done on my return to Canada at the end of my posting in the summer of 2015. Unfortunately, it was not very successful either, despite an excellent physio in Ottawa, also for several months. As a result, I cannot straighten that arm, but the good news is I can still do most of the things I like to do such as swimming, cycling and kayaking. And so, I am slightly twisted physically now as well as in my kinky personality – I am harmonized!

Leaving Haiti was sweet sorrow. It was time, and it had been a lovely ride. In many ways it was a great last posting. It was my longest and, in some ways, my most normal overseas adventure. It was not Paris or London as my mother had wished for me, but it was probably more my cup of tea anyway. I have always been attracted to the unusual – maybe it is where I fit in best.

Epilogue

Despite **my quirky inclinations**, I have ended up happily ensconced in Canada's most British city, Victoria, at the southern end of Vancouver Island. Some say Canada's West Coast is its best coast but I'm sure there are others who dispute that. Of course, I am not one of them. I appreciate the moderate climate, which usually brings us spring in early February. And then spring just keeps on giving, well into May when the rest of Canada is valiantly trying to catch up to our brilliant blossom displays. The ocean air exhilarates my senses and the waterfront walks enthral me with beachcombing and marvelous views over the Salish Sea to the Olympic Mountains of Washington State.

Following my three-year posting in Haiti, I returned to headquarters in Ottawa to spend another year on the Haiti program there. It allowed me to get re-acquainted with my Ottawa friends, although I was busy downsizing in preparation to sell my home.

I retired in mid-August 2016 and a month later headed west to drive across our wonderful country to my new home in Victoria. Coincidentally, Victoria Sutherland, a friend who had been my boss at one point, offered to accompany me as far as Calgary before she flew back to Ottawa. We took our time, stopping to visit friends and family along the way. It was a lovely gradual approach to the current chapter of my life.

The Newcomers Club of Greater Victoria and the Unitarians here have smoothed my entry to a happy and fulfilling life in Victoria. I have now lived here longer than in any other location since leaving Ottawa for Kandahar in the summer of 2008. I just might be settled, finally!

About the Author

| Teens | 20s | 30s | 40s | 50s | 60s |

Karen Christie is an intrepid adventurer, whose innate curiosity has taken her to six of the world's seven continents. She began that life-long journey as a teacher in remote corners, and ended her career as a diplomat representing Canada in a couple of tough insecure countries. She is now happily retired in Victoria, BC, Canada, where she revels in the year-round glory of the gardens, and the majestic beauty of the Salish Sea.